Vermont Ain't for Sissies

A Woman's Journey

By

Elaine Polson Shiber

authorHOUSE™

1663 LIBERTY DRIVE, SUITE 200
BLOOMINGTON, INDIANA 47403
(800) 839-8640
WWW.AUTHORHOUSE.COM

First published by AuthorHouse 05/17/05

ISBN: 1-4208-2527-5 (sc)

Printed in the United States of America
Bloomington, Indiana

This book is printed on acid-free paper.

Cover design by Carole Shiber.

This book is for Warren, and for
his grandchildren, Darcy, Aaron and
Faith, who never had the pleasure
of knowing him. Now they will.

CONTENTS

PROLOGUE

IT WAS ONE OF THE BEST THINGS I've ever done but for a long time I didn't think so.

In 1974 my husband and I moved from Long Island to Vermont. We put our Massapequa split-level house on the market, packed up most of our belongings and all of who we were and ran away to our vacation home in Vermont without making too many plans.

We lived there for ten years.

I was born in Brooklyn, grew up on Long Island, graduated from Baldwin High School, went to a secretarial school in New York City, and then commuted on the Long Island Railroad every day to work there.

Warren was born and grew up in Wilkes Barre, Pennsylvania, tried out a few colleges, and somehow made his way to Baldwin where we discovered each other.

We married after a respectable amount of time and later bought a house in Nassau Shores, Massapequa, where we raised two daughters for a while.

We lived a life of triumphs and failures, and when our kids went off to college, one at a time, we figured we'd settle back, put our feet up and begin to take life easy.

That never happened, because if it had we never would have ended up living in Vermont.

The thought of spending the rest of our days in suburbia doing the required suburban thing—living in the perfect house with the perfect lawn on the perfect block—was beginning to look unappealing. Our child-rearing responsibilities were behind us, and as seasoned Long Islanders, we had to be in pain at least part of the time. We didn't plan it that way but it turned out we exchanged the pain of Long Island for the pain of Vermont.

Why did we move to Vermont? It's simple when you see how very Type A we were. We'd built a vacation house there, and the idea of moving to Vermont was exciting. We had reached the Old and Bored stage in our lives and were ready for the New and Challenging. Aha! How much do we know about Vermont? Not much. Let's go!

Thus begins the tale of how two tall, normal-looking New-York-City-loving people just up and left the paved madness of Long Island and trekked north to the peaceful, isolated beauty of Vermont, set up housekeeping and somehow survived. One of them even lived to tell about it.

The one who was a sissy. Yop! I was a tall, normal-looking sissy from Long Island. Raised in a Swedish-American home. Swedish. As in Viking. Where had my plundering and looting Viking blood gone? *Now* was when I needed it.

I thought I was a toughie back there on Long Island. But I soon found out I was nothing but a sissy when I got to Vermont, and Vermont ain't for sissies.

Stay tuned.

VACATIONS NOW. RETIREMENT LATER.

HOW DO YOU GET FROM Long Island to Vermont?

Let's see. You can cogitate. You can hesitate. You can emigrate. We did each of those in time. But first we went by way of Pennsylvania.

I'll take you back to the nineteen-fifties when Warren and I knew someday we'd be old and funny in the head and body and ready to retire. Even though we hadn't hit forty yet, we saw that the smarties were busy making nest-egg plans.

Warren was self-employed as an auto mechanic and body repair man. In 1952, our first baby, Christine, was born, but Warren already had a "baby" of his own, a fiberglass sports car he'd designed and built from scratch. He tried to market it without success, but when Chevrolet introduced the fiberglass Corvette in the mid-fifties, Warren had already learned the fine art of fiberglass fabrication and repair and could easily put back into shape any smashed Corvette body on Long Island.

And put them back together again he did and then some. He soon had a few Corvette owners who wanted to race the amateur sports car circuit from New England to Florida. This group of guys became Team Shiber, each with his own Corvette and a jacket inscribed with his own name. The venture gave Warren a good income and lots of fun but no pension plan. My jobs as full-time wife and mother and part-time church volunteer didn't even give me an income, let alone pension plans.

What to do? Hey! Idea! Let's buy some property somewhere off Long Island, build a house on it when we save some money, and when we're ready to retire, we'll be all set. It sounds kinda nuts now that I'm in my seventies and Warren left this life in his fifties, but at the time we were smug with our smarts.

Elaine Polson Shiber

We started looking for our dream property in Pennsylvania and wound up buying property in Vermont a few years later.

What I remember about that trip to the Poconos was the sweet smell of pine, the sun trying to work its way through the trees and the big thud of disappointment in the pit of my stomach. Warren had grown up in Pennsylvania, and when his cousin Dorothy, a real estate broker, said, "I just found two parcels in Bear Creek," Warren was ready to jump in the car and go buy both of them.

Bear Creek was too rich for our wallet. We came home, faced financial reality and temporarily shelved plans for our future.

Let's move on to the sixties. That's when our friends the Gallaghers told us all about their recent pack trip on horses in Vermont.

4

MOONLIGHT IN VERMONT

I HAVE TROUBLE WITH THE NOTION that anyone who's a friend of mine would take a trip on a horse. Car? Bus? Train? Boat? Yes. A horse? Never.

But our friends Ida Jane and Jack Gallagher wouldn't have found Beebe Pond if they hadn't been on horses.

Both of them had grown up in West Virginia where I guess there are a lot of horses. No? There aren't a lot of horses in West Virginia? It's Virginia that has the horses? Oh. Maybe it was because they were athletic and liked to climb to the top of a horse? And were outdoorsy besides the horse thing? They *looked* athletic, being sleek and trim and all that. But come to think of it, I'd never heard them talk about horses. So when they told us about their trip on horses and their guide pointing out to them that "jewel of a lake" beneath them when they got to Eagle Rock, I *was* rather suspicious. But I had to believe them. They wouldn't make it up about the horses.

Horses or not, one night they described that jewel of a lake to us and told us about June Sherline, the owner of all the surrounding property and how they bought 15 acres from her and were having a cabin built and why didn't we drive up and see it? Weren't we looking for an investment property to build a house on? To retire to? And anyway June Sherline has lots of land left. C'mon up!

We succumbed to their wiles. Late in the summer of 1964 Ida Jane and Jack gave us detailed directions and we looked at a map and planned our weekend outing. Our older daughter Chris was almost a teenager and stayed at a friend's house, and Carole, the daughter who joined us almost three years after Chris, loved leaving her sister home and going off with her folks. We had a new Corvette Stingray (silver) and there was just

5

enough room for a nine-year-old to fold herself into the space behind the front seats, despite her long legs.

Honest, we planned on leaving Saturday morning, early, so we could get to the Gallaghers before noon but we'd never asked them how long it would take to drive there. But, heck, if we left when Warren got home from work on Friday, think how much more time we could spend in Vermont! I made what I'm sure were sandwiches with peanut butter and no flair but I'm also sure I tucked in potato chips and Fritos to make up for the plain main offering. And Yankee Doodles.

It was still light when we left Massapequa on that glorious summer evening, but by the time we crossed the Vermont state line it was very late and very dark.

It took us about six hours to get where we finally got. Where? There. The excitement and anticipation were wearing off until we spotted the moon rising.

"Boy, what a night! Look at that moon!"

"Moonlight in Vermont, what makes it seem so exciting!"

Humming filled the car. La de da de da de da de. How romantic! We were giddy with the thrill of it all. We calculated it should take another hour to reach Beebe Pond, although the Gallaghers weren't expecting to see us at *any* hour on Friday. (What were we *thinking?*)

It was so dark. Darker than I had ever seen dark. Street lights? Not where *we* were. Maybe in Vermont towns with more than 8,000 people but, alas, not on Route 30. We got to the creep-along stage once we hit the nine-mile mark of the required ten miles. We were on a two-lane road and all we could make out were unlimited collections of tall black trees, singles and in groups. Once in a while a darkened house. It was probably 11 p.m. and Vermont had gone to bed by now, and by now we weren't having a good time.

The Vermont moonlight was still with us, though, and as I watched with increasing alarm its relentless path west, I was able to share with the driver that we might be lost. Suddenly what to our wondering eyes should appear but a tiny sign. With nothing on it that we recognized, however.

"Stop!" I cried. "That could be it! No. It says Lake Hortonia. Two miles that way. But we don't want Lake Hortonia. We want Beebe Pond. Could that have been what we passed a few minutes ago?"

Warren muttered something. I saw that he didn't want to play Twenty Questions.

We drove back. And forth. And back again. The driver was getting testy. The other front-seater was getting testy. The third passenger had fallen asleep long ago, probably back there in New York State.

"Oh, Lord. Know what time it is?" I was looking at the watch I loved to push the button on so I could see the dial in the dark.

"You'd better tell me."

"It's just past midnight. We can't go to the Gallaghers now. Even if we could find them. They'll be asleep. Let's try to find a motel." She said simply.

"Oh, sure. A motel. HAVE YOU SEEN ANYTHING THAT LOOKS LIKE A MOTEL IN THIS GODFORSAKEN PLACE?"

Our nerves were shot. We were cranky. I noted the lack of the moonlight song.

We pulled on to the first dirt road we could make out in the dark, parked way over in the grass, and slept in the car.

By the time the sun came up over Eagle Rock, on the top of the mountain next to us and across the road, we were sleeping soundly. Once we opened our eyes and realized we were where we were supposed to be—there was the big brown sign with the big white letters EAGLE ROCK ESTATES—(how could we have missed it? Ha!)—we felt silly.

Silly and happy, and stiff from avoiding the gearshift sticking up between us for those few short but long hours.

"I'm hungry." Carole. Wide awake, bushy-tailed and ready to eat.

Breakfast?   Breakfast?   NOW it was time to drop in on the Gallaghers!

DOES A LONG ISLANDER PEE IN THE WOODS?

"WE'RE LOOKING FOR THE GALLAGHERS," Warren said to the first person we saw. The woman was walking her dog along the road.

"You mean the Intrepid Ones?" Because I wasn't forty yet, I didn't know what that meant until I looked it up in my Funk & Wagnalls when we got home. "Unshaken by fear; dauntless; bold; brave."

It was early morning and it was June Sherline with the dog. June is the special woman who was developing the property around Beebe Pond. She smiled broadly despite the hour and told us where we could find our friends.

Up near the sky at the top of a "driveway" *this* Long Islander would never have attempted to drive up (but the former Pennsylvanian had no trouble), we found Ida Jane, Jack, and their two kids, Nancy and John. And Gypsy, their Dalmatian, who recognized us and wagged her tail while she barked.

Their house had been framed but we couldn't help notice the absence of siding. We could look from the back to the front of the house without pausing. Inside we saw two tents, one in the "living room" and one in one of the "bedrooms."

"Intrepid" was an apt description, I found out later. The Gallaghers were camping out not just with a roof over their heads but with two doors, one in front and one on the side. When it rained they didn't have to close the windows. There weren't any.

They fed us, of course. The smell of the bacon and eggs frying still lingers. The coffee was hot and there was lots of it. There's something very special about breakfast in the woods. (Or at the beach. Or in a restaurant. I've never really met a breakfast out I didn't like.)

9

We were told if we had to use the bathroom, that little three by three enclosed room over there held a porta-potty if we *really* needed it, but then they told us peeing is done in the woods.

Uh oh. I'd been peeing in the ocean all my life but when I sneaked a peek at the woods that morning they looked mysterious and ominous to eyes unaccustomed to woods. When I couldn't hold out any longer, I figured, what the heck. Warren walked out first, and when he came back Carole and I casually wandered out through the clearing and did what had to be done, the two of us checking out the flora and fauna before squatting behind two big old trees. Warren the country boy found this all very natural but Carole and I braved those woods only once more until we stopped at a gas station on the way home.

We liked what we saw that day. We walked and we walked and we even took a swim in the lake without peeing because we were told we weren't allowed because some camp owners used the lake water for drinking, forsooth. The Gallaghers filled us in on land prices. We liked the lake, the trees, the terrain, the clean, clear air. It all felt good and this was definitely a possibility for vacations-now and retirement-later.

We were ready to consider Vermont.

. . . AND HAVE YOU EVER SMELLED SUCH AIR?

THE NEXT TIME WE drove up we knew how long six hours can take. We left on time on Friday. Found out there was one motel in Castleton. Made a reservation. Made an appointment with June Sherline to see some properties. Had bacon and eggs and all the rest at the Castleton Diner. And took both kids.

June drove us in her station wagon, Warren and she in the front seat and her Doberman sharing the back seats with the kids and me. She showed us several sites but none came up to what we thought we were looking for. We left June and drove up that Godawful hill again to see the Gallaghers. They were having coffee with Al Greeley, the all-weather, all-knowing, all-Vermonter-from-way-back Beebe Pond entrepreneur and June's side-kick.

Al was also a wonderful story-teller and colorful character. He was of medium height and weight, more husky and lean than medium, if you know what I mean. His hair was light brown with a sprinkling of gray at the temples. He was clean shaven and he was wearing a faded brown cotton porkpie hat almost squarely on his head, except he had turned the brim down just so over one eye. And he smelled good. He had that clean, soapy smell as if he had come right here from the shower. That was the smell that I recognized in many of the "real" Vermonters I met through the years. I loved that smell, and when I catch a whiff of it today, I think of Vermont and Al Greeley.

I want to pause here to tell you about Al's distinctive language. He had once described to Ida Jane and Jack a house on the other side of the lake as the "Christly" house, as in Jesus Christ-ly. It took most of us a while to figure out that's what he meant.

11

There were some regional differences afoot here. Although New York touches Vermont just above Albany and continues on up to the Canadian border, and even if the two states share Lake Champlain, I could see some differences in our ways of thinking and speaking, right down to swear words.

Vermonters approach life differently. They take more time to figure things out than I do. Until I got used to that, I was impatient with their patience. I wanted things done yesterday. They, on the other hand, appeared to have more time just to *be*. When I became aware of this new idea and was able to relax, I tried it on and it felt good. But my impatience is part of my being raised on Long Island (in addition to my visible Type A birthright) and it never left me entirely. But at least I recognized it as *my* problem.

At first, though, they had my number. Our different ways of handling situations caused me grief occasionally and I was homesick for the old New-York-Minute pace. C'mon! Get on with it!

Warren, on the other hand, having grown up in Pennsylvania, was closer to Vermont in spirit than I was. He could talk to a new Vermont friend in an unhurried way and this must have been pleasing to his new neighbors. He and another guy would stand facing each other, each looking down at the ground, neither talking. They would kind of kick the dirt around with the toes of their boots while slowly pondering what to say next. That drove me crazy. (Maybe I just needed to buy some boots.)

Warren was easing himself into his new home environment without much of a ripple but I know I was just a big pain in the ass, with my hurry hurry attitude. When I realized how pushy I was, I stopped to look at what was going on around me and talked to some of my Long Island friends about my observations. I'd seen people in other parts of the country taking in newcomers to their hearts and homes readily, without reservation. It was "Hi!" and "Welcome!" with nary a thought behind it, or so I thought.

But Vermonters——Calvin Coolidge came from Vermont——are more wary and need time to size up newcomers for a while. They hold judgment in abeyance, both good and bad. When a newcomer is accepted, however, there is nothing that Vermonter won't do for his new friend, no matter what that person does. A commendable quality, I think.

Back to Al Greeley. He spoke to the Gallaghers about that "Christly" (as in Jesus, just to remind you) house that was awful and one no self-respecting Vermonter would own. He said a flatlander from New Jersey had bought the land and then had that ugly house built on it.

A few weeks later, Ida Jane was rowing her boat around the lake. She spotted a man standing on the deck of the house Al had described. Friendly Ida Jane was eager to meet her new neighbor. She pulled up to the nearest dock, tied up her rowboat and walked up the path to the man on his deck. Ida Jane is a sweet and friendly woman, and can be somewhat trusting and naïve. As she approached her new neighbor, she called out to him, "Mr. Christly?"

Ida Jane didn't hesitate to share her embarrassment with the rest of us later. The man immediately told her what his name was, and in that moment she got it. Of course the Wolons house would be known as the Christly house forevermore.

Back to my story before the detour. As it happened, Al owned a piece of property which he'd advertised for sale in the *Rutland Herald* that day. He asked if we wanted to see it. He told us that several years earlier he had cut a road in around the lake for June's enterprise. They had agreed she would pay him in a lovely piece of land with 300 feet of lakefront. The property had about 2-1/2 acres with it and the mountainside climbed rather quickly up the hill from the road.

Al wanted to sell the parcel and we were willing to take a look. He led us down from the Gallaghers through the woods and undergrowth and laid out for us in our imaginations the driveway as it circled up one side and down the other. He pointed out the possible site for the camp (the Vermont word for cabin) adjacent to the driveway. Then he walked us just south of the camp site to point out the "perfect spot for your picnic table." It was this last that pushed these gullible Long Island folks right over the edge to Purchase Ville. He was GOOD! The four of us looked at each other and grinned.

A few months later we owned a piece of Vermont.

... And have you ever smelled such air?

TWO PACKS OF CIGARETTES

THAT'S WHAT WARREN USED to design our cabin in the Vermont woods.

Many nights at our kitchen table in Massapequa that next winter, after the dishes were done and the kids were upstairs doing their homework, we'd put our heads and cigarette packs together and make plans.

Warren placed those packs—-his manly Marlboros and my lady-like king-size filter-tip Kents in the flip-top box—-just so. One pack (mine) was the 24 x 36 foot basic Gallagher floor plan. The other one (his) was the addition we would put on which would extend over the proposed driveway. We were dreaming far into the future with that second pack but that idea never became a reality. We went sideways instead when we enlarged the existing house. Designing a house with cigarette packs allows you to change your mind.

I found some graph paper and laid out the rooms in the basic house: large living/dining room/kitchen. Bathroom. Three bedrooms across the back. Simple and sweet. Casual but efficient. Perfect for vacations-now.

That was in 1966. We didn't start to build until 1969.

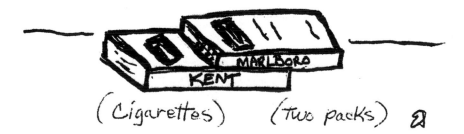

(Cigarettes)   (Two packs)

Elaine Polson Shiber

DON'T FORGET YOUR TOWEL!

I CAN STILL SMELL ALL THOSE SMELLS! The smell of the Gallagher house, the smell of the woods surrounding their house, the smell of the dampness as the fallen leaves were kicked up as we walked, the fresh smell of the lake if we were in it or on it, the smell of the fire in their fireplace on a chilly August morning, and the distinctive stagnant smell of the water as we bailed it out of their rowboat. And of course that air I seldom smell any more unless I go to Vermont to visit Lake Beebe, which is what we later called it.

Ida Jane and Jack generously lent us their camp for a long weekend or two each summer after we bought the land. We were still in the dreaming stages and needed to check on our piece of Vermont. It wasn't going anywhere but kept growing more spruce trees and aspens nonetheless. All those trees made us happy because we loved trees and plenty of 'em. Then.

Their house was in the sky--the third tier up from the lake. Our piece was the second tier, and the first tier bordered the lake. Going back up again, there was the lake, then the road, then our land, then way up there was the Gallaghers. Whenever we spent a long weekend in their cabin during the summer it was an easy walk down to the lake for a swim.

But don't forget your towel!

THE BACK BURNER

FOR THOSE THREE YEARS, from the time we bought the land until we were able to put something on it, we were pretty busy back there in Massapequa. There were jobs and automobile racing and cleaning and cooking and sewing and decorating and throwing parties and mowing the lawn and planting flowers after all danger of frost was past and sitting around most Saturday nights for warm and stimulating gabfests with good friends and parenting two great kids and helping with homework if we were asked and singing in the choir and attending church board meetings and doing Christmas and Halloween and the Fourth of July and early Sunday morning breakfasts at Field 9 at Jones Beach and going to the movies and shoveling snow and ice-skating on Caroons Lake and approving of our kids' dates and disapproving of our kids' dates and dancing at weddings and shopping. We had little time to think about our piece of Vermont most days. Then something happened to bring our future into the present.

In June 1969 Warren's mother died, and his father Harold, after an intense period of mourning, and after some serious thought, came down from his home in Massachusetts to Long Island to make us an offer. He thought it might be good for all of us—-therapy for him and a vacation home for us-—if he started to build our cabin in Vermont. He came from a family of building contractors and knew what he would be undertaking. He was also anxious to start feeling useful again. It didn't take us too long to say, yes, that would be a worthwhile project for him and for us. It was time for us to put Vermont on a front burner.

Warren, never one to let grass grow under either of his feet, knew immediately how he was going to use those panes of 12 x 24 inch glass in those boxes hanging around in the shop he was renting for his business in Westbury. He designed on paper an 18 foot long by 12 foot high window which would overlook the lake. (And, Al, just to the left of the picnic table, okay?) Picture a partitioned liquor box which goes on and on and you have a slight idea of what that window frame looked like. The panes of glass would be placed with one on the outside of the partition and one on the inside, with about eight inches in between, which theoretically would create double-glazing for insulation. Of course, neither of us had taken one Vermont winter into consideration, but when the sun was shining it was grand and toasty in the house. And the window was beautiful to look at when it was snowing.

While that window was being constructed by the Brandon Lumber Yard in Vermont (the glass would be inserted by Warren one weekend in the fall when the frame was delivered and in place), we made further plans for the house we'd been designing with cigarette packs and graph paper.

Harold was anxious to get on with our house. And his life.

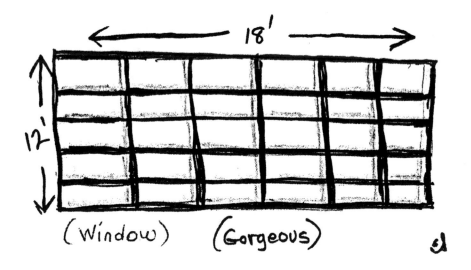

(Window) (Gorgeous)

GO JUMP IN THE LAKE!

WE DIDN'T WASTE ANY TIME. We knew the building season for that year in Vermont was fast coming to a close.

Warren and I went up one weekend in August to site the house. The suggestion to remove a large number of those fast-growing spruces and aspens before any structure went up met with the disapproval of these environmentally conscious but dumb Long Islanders.

"Cut down a lot of trees? Are you crazy? We want you to clear just the area where the cabin will go!" But it wasn't too many years later we regretted our reluctance to get rid of the excess trees. We sweated every time a felled tree barely missed the cabin as it came down. After living in a house where trees kept ganging up on us, we finally admitted we needed more light.

As soon as Warren could enlist the aid of two of his Corvette-racing buddies, Bert Green the Builder, and Mike Mandell the Willing, the three men and I drove up one Friday night in early September to meet Warren's father. Harold had already done the foundation work to Warren's and his specifications. My two Shiber men had made a lumber list, and when we drove up the hill, there were all those boards just sitting there waiting to be seen, or, uh, sawed.

Friends of ours from Massapequa, Dot and Ed Von Rhee, who owned the house on the tier just above us, had offered us their place for the weekend. We slept and ate there for two days and three nights while our cabin was being framed.

It was agreed Bert would supervise the job. He was the pro, the real builder with his own business in Bellmore, Long Island. Bert did the final act of the rough framing: he hung the two outside doors, one in front and one on the side. It was understood not just any old guy could hang an exterior door, so we all stood around and watched Bert do his stuff.

Mike volunteered to do the roofing because he was afraid of snakes. He was also afraid of heights. He chose the lesser of two evils?

Do you know what a chicken coop looks like? It sounds funny, but Warren designed the house like a chicken coop, country boy that he was. The roof slanted back from a high front of maybe 14 feet to about 10 feet in the back. (All measurements are approximate and not to be taken too seriously.) On this score, Warren had indeed been thinking of the Vermont winters when he designed the house. Any snow could easily slide off the roof with a little help. I think Mike also had fears of sliding off the roof with no help at all whenever he had to move around doing his roofing job. Once he got the hang of hanging on, though, he liked looking down on us. After a while he even got good at waving with one hand while hanging on with the rest of him.

I prepared the meals—breakfast and lunch anyway-—and I'm sure we ate dinner out each night because we'd found some neat restaurants in the area. One morning Mike wanted to help me with breakfast. In his haste to get back to his roof, he opened the refrigerator door, quickly grabbed the carton of orange juice and immediately dropped it on the floor. The carton had already been opened, so almost a half gallon of juice spread quickly throughout the area without pausing. When the guys went off to work, hi ho hi ho, I got down on my hands and knees and did my best to mop up the mess. But when Mike came back in later, his boots stuck to the floor with every step, so he finished what I thought I'd finished. I never told Dot and Ed what we did to their floor, and I don't plan to tell them the next time I see them either.

I also did the go-fering that weekend when we forgot or needed something from the store, like another half gallon of orange juice.

The workers stopped working those two days just to eat lunch and catch their breath now and then. When Sunday night came they were pretty tired, but when someone yelled, "Go jump in the lake!" they weren't too tired to do just that, clothes and all.

I got the towels. And joined them. Clothes and all.

It was one of the best swims I've ever had.

LAKE BEEBE. FIRST FRAMING.

LAKE BEEBE. Rough siding begins.

LET US GIVE THANKS!

"OH, THAT MUST BE IT! He left the light on for us!"

It was the night before Thanksgiving 1969. Harold had gone back to Massachusetts for the holiday weekend. It was the first time we'd been back to Vermont since the big framing weekend. We were excited.

After we'd left that Monday morning in September, Harold had stayed on and continued to complete the rest of our plans. He'd bought a used dark blue Ford Econoline and had outfitted it with a sleeping bag and mattress. He had installed a porta-potty and a small Sterno-powered cookstove. He'd parked the van at the top of the driveway, which had been created earlier by a crew of earth-movers with heavy equipment and backhoes. He made the van his lonely home until the cabin was ready for him to move into.

Harold worked solo through the rest of September and all of October, except when he'd arranged for Bill Steele to install the circuit breaker panel box. Bill was a licensed Vermont electrician and was fast becoming a good friend of ours. Harold could then complete the wiring.

Other neighbors on the lake, Jody and Nick Zeoli, had taken Harold under their wings and were feeding him some fine home-cooked meals whenever they came up from Connecticut for a fall weekend. Harold told us it was a welcome break-—not to mention good company—-live!-—from his usual Chef Boyardee spaghetti and Dinty Moore corned beef hash, his favorites when he wasn't invited to dine out.

Harold was in constant telephone contact with us. He told us he thought he would be ready to show off his and our pride and joy by Thanksgiving.

We didn't drive the Corvette this time, so Chris and Carole didn't have to crowd themselves behind the front seats. There was plenty of room in the back of our old Oldsmobile for them to pinch each other—-or sleep when they got tired of doing that. The kids hadn't even seen the framing done, so they were pretty excited, too.

As we made our way along the lake road, we suddenly saw the lights through those hundreds of spruce and aspen trees still standing. There it was! What had been a wooden skeleton with two doors and a roof was now an honest-to-God full-blown cabin with windows and lamps and everything. There was even a stove-pipe sticking out of the roof!

We had agreed that Harold would leave the key over the front door (you gotta watch those raccoons). After bumping into each other in our excitement and in the dark, we finally got the door unlocked and the four of us now slipped into a hushed mood of anticipation. We seemed to be tiptoeing into the living room.

The feeling that came over me then is one I can still feel these many years later. What we'd been imagining and planning had become real and touchable. The house was warm, thanks to the electric heat, and the house was wonderful. We had trouble believing our eyes and simply sat down on the nearest chairs Harold had brought in and began oohing and aahing whenever something new caught our eye.

Harold had put up the exterior siding, installed mega amounts of insulation, and, of course, there was that dramatic 18 x 12 foot window all finished and set in place and overlooking the lake. That night we could just make out the undisturbed and placid almost-frozen lake through the trees even in the dark. That was the absolute focal point and it took our breath away.

He had finished the walls and the floors and had hung doors to the three bedrooms along the back. He'd made a real bathroom with a stall shower, a toilet and a sink, and had hung another door so no one could come in unannounced. There was a kitchen sink with a four by six window above it, also facing the lake, with rough-built counters. He'd put in a brand new electric stove and a brand new copper-colored refrigerator (which was so *chi-chi* in those days) with a freezer along the side. The two appliances matched! Then he had some time left over and added a few homey touches, like a shelf here and a shelf there on which he'd placed a few of his precious knickknacks from home. Baskets and candle holders were a special touch.

Warren lit a fire in the new Franklin stove with the newspaper and kindling which were nearby. He'd already nicknamed the Franklin stove The Benny (you know, after Benny Franklin, who invented it) a few years earlier on our vacations to Maine.

We probably got to sleep sometime during the night but I don't remember what we slept on. What I do remember is that we paused many times to give thanks to God for His providence. And for Harold and his hard and lonely work.

LAKE BEEBE. Phase One finished.

VACATIONS NOW!
RETIREMENT—-NOW?

THE "VACATIONS NOW!" part of those plans we'd been busy making had finally arrived.

We spent the New Year of 1970 in a couple of feet of fresh white snow. The road around the lake had been cleared, thanks to Bill Steele, so we parked at the bottom of our driveway, and because the kids were young and we were younger than we'd ever be again, we got up that hill without too much trouble. We had eight hands to carry the supplies for the weekend into the cabin.

There were a few other families vacationing on the lake, too, so we had a rip-roaring social time of it. I took a picture of the HAPPY NEW YEAR we wrote in the deep snow on the hill in front of the house. That was the start of our VACATIONS NOW.

Our kids were soon to be 18 and 15 and we found it hard to get them to join us on a Vermont vacation unless we agreed to bring some of their friends along. So VACATIONS-NOW was mostly just Warren and me trekking northward, not minding giving up our mad, mad Long Island life now and then and basking in the peaceful beauty of Vermont. Besides, an occasional mini-honeymoon seemed to agree with us. When we weren't honeymooning or fighting, we played house and smoothed out some of the existing rough edges in the cabin. We swam in the lake-—even skinny-dipped one summer day at high noon on a cloudy Wednesday (when no one was around). We liked to hike and found trails and glens and explored as many as we found. We cooked and drank and entertained, and we were also entertained by our lake neighbors and beyond.

We weren't giving RETIREMENT-LATER another thought at the moment.

It's funny how 1974 snuck up on us. Chris had just graduated from Cornell and was heading west to attend the Pacific School of Religion in Berkeley, California. Carole was starting her second year at the University of Vermont in Burlington.

The nest was emptying.

"RETIREMENT-LATER!" Now?

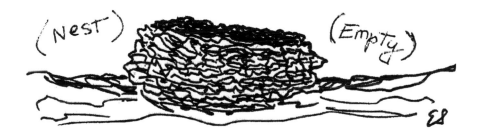

PLAN AHEA D

IN THE GLOVE COMPARTMENT OF MY CAR is an envelope holding a bunch of three by five cards. On each I've written directions to anywhere I've driven or am planning to drive in the future.

Planning and being prepared is one of my endearing compulsive qualities. I keep the current travel card close to me, either on the seat beside me or in my hand if I'm getting close to where I'm going. On the card I write down the destination. The numbers of the routes I'll be taking. The approximate length of time I'll be driving. I leave nothing to chance when I start out on the road. I have a full tank of gas and I feel good because—-dammit—-I'm prepared. The envelope has become shabby over time, and I've just moved it to the side pocket of my latest car. On the outside of the envelope is written in bold magic marker, DIRECTIONS TO EVERYWHERE.

However, the narrative I'm about to relate will show you the exception that proves my rule.

In 1974, Warren and I finally said RETIREMENT-LATER is RETIREMENT-NOW, and you'll see that RETIREMENT-NOW was actually MOVE-NOW. Retirement never happened. (And still hasn't.)

When we moved ten years after buying the land and five years after building the basic house, we just, well, packed up and moved. There wasn't a map for the initial trip because we already knew the way. Did we have a map for when we got there? Nope. We had made no plans whatsoever. Nada. Zip.

Our friends thought it was Warren's idea to move to Vermont. He was the country boy, wasn't he? But I was the other half of an impulsive couple and I'd become restless. I gave my impulsive side free rein one day and asked Warren, "How would you like to move to Vermont?" He was restless, too, no doubt. It took him less than a minute to answer, "Why not?"

It seemed like the right time. Both kids had flown the coop, one in seminary and one in college. The gasoline shortage of 1974 was putting a crimp in Warren's auto racing business and we couldn't see around the corner into our financial future. And gee! When we sold our house we'd have "all that money" to live on. And wasn't it going to be cheaper to live in Vermont than it was living on Long Island? (One day after we'd lived there a while, I said, "I know why it's cheaper to live in Vermont. Ya can't BUY anything!") Okay, so now we were willing to leave the suburbs and to try our hand at country living. *Green Acres* was beckoning us.

Is everyone in their late forties so devil-may-care? So what-the-hell? We hadn't given too much thought as to how we'd make a living. Oh, a little, but thoughts were fleeting and minimal. I never wrote down on a three by five card the possibilities for work or any doubts we might have about leaving the neighborhood and old friends and the church and the life we'd gotten used to and loved. We were young. We were ready for a challenge, and we never considered the risks. Or anything else for that matter.

We sold our house, had a garage sale in our garage a week before we moved. We rented the biggest, ugliest red Hub truck available and packed it with the rest of our belongings with the help of family and friends.

October 1974 was fast drawing to a close. Winter in Vermont was just around the corner but what did we know? Or care?

As we drove slowly away from our Massapequa home in that big, ugly red and white truck, turning right and heading north into our future, we were filled with wondrous anticipation.

But suddenly I was filled with something else that was slowly but definitely creeping up from my gut. I identified it later as homesickness.

I was going to have lots and lots of time to deal with that little number once we got to Vermont.

Warren holding up Hub Truck

WE'RE JUST A COUPLE OF SWELLS!

THAT WAS THE SONG WE SANG as we rolled merrily——and not a little soberly——northward to Vermont.

By the time we pulled on to the dirt road leading to our house and drove steadily to our destination, guiltily knocking down low-hanging tree branches as we inched slowly onward, because it had become November in Vermont, it was dark, it was cold and we were tired.

Warren coaxed that big unwieldy truck up the narrow, rutted driveway behind the house after several tries, and the lights from the house beamed a golden glow of welcome through the by-now millions of spruce and aspen trees. Harold and his friend Jen had gotten there earlier from Massachusetts and had dinner waiting for us. We entered our new home——and our new life——with a whoop!

It was then that I heard the bang of the door slamming shut behind us. Or was it the sound of the sawed-off limb crashing to the ground——with us on it? Or it may have been the roar of the burning bridge back there on Long Island.

It could have been all three.

I know it was very loud.

HOME, JAMES!

I'D PROBABLY DECIDED those first few months in Vermont were worth some serious reality blurring. We were so busy being busy with unpacking and getting over colds and settling into our new life that we had run out of brains. Shortly after our arrival, we'd found an old farmhouse *right away* up the road a piece and bought it *immediately* to renovate *at once*. This would give us something to do. And do. And *do*. Homesickness wouldn't be able to find us, we'd be so busy.

One night in late January, the two of us stood holding on to each other (for dear life) in front of the dramatic 18 by 12 foot window overlooking the bleak and frozen lake. We were watching the snow as it fell--and fell--and fell. As we turned our heads to look to either side of our snug little house, we could see only the darkened and vacant vacation homes through the trunks of those *billions* of tall, beautiful snow-covered spruce and aspen trees. Looking out in front of us across frozen Lake Beebe, we could make out the occasional teeny tiny yellow headlights moving slowly, slowly up or down Route 30 through the falling snow. It was so quiet. Quiet we weren't used to. I mean, really quiet.

Warren sighed then, once and again——big sighs--and that's when he turned to me and said, "Well, this has been a nice vacation Let's go home now."

WHITING

HOME IS WHERE THE HEART IS, as the adage goes. Our hearts were back on Long Island but our home was now the snug little house on Lake Beebe. And had we forgotten about that other house in the town of Whiting that we'd bought in November right after we hit town? The one we could be busy renovating by using our building skills? We were stuck, you might say. Now we owned not one but two houses in Vermont. And neither one felt like "home." "Well!" as Stan Laurel (or Oliver Hardy) used to say, "A fine mess you've gotten us into."

Here was our first close-up look at New and Challenging at last. Here we were, smack dab in the middle of Vermont with winter already upon us. Cold? Yes. Boring? No.

Time to test our city-slicker smarts. Along with his automobile savvy, Warren had been doing carpentry work since the age of 12 when he took shop at school. I had inherited my father's love of wallpapering, painting and decorating of all kinds. For years I'd been a decorating fool. I was Martha Stewart before she was--but I never did any investing.

The only way through this was to go through it. And the way through it was to get busy and go to work.

Money + Skills + Will = Work. We had "all that money" from the sale of the old homestead on Long Island. We had skills we hadn't tapped yet (we hoped). Lord knows we had enough will and daring to try anything. And our need to return to sanity must have figured in that equation somewhere, too.

When we saw the FOR SALE sign in front of a sad-looking old house on the west side of Route 30 in Whiting, 10 miles north of Lake Beebe, our guts said BUY!

This old house will hereinafter be referred to as "Whiting." It was easier to name our possessions than to refer to them as "the house we're working on" or "that place up the road," or blah blah blah.

We spent all of $12,000 (cash!) of our new-found wealth on an old, faded red, two-story farmhouse (with potential). Upon inspection before the closing, we found a kitchen with a brand new white electric stove, and counters which were going south. Just off the kitchen was a huge room, formerly used, we guessed from the smell, for animals. It then became a huge room in which to store the rest of our furniture until we decided where to put it all. (Remember PLAN AHEA D?)

Going in another direction from the kitchen, there was a living room casually arranged with a dining area--around the corner of a partition—which could also be reached from the kitchen if we put a door in between. The dining area featured, right in the middle where a drop-leaf table would eventually go, a brand new off white oil burner. Right off the kitchen and against the living room wall climbed a staircase with almost a full set of steps (there were a few gaps) going up to three bedrooms, or rather, the three bedrooms we'd create. Underneath all this was a smelly dank cellar with an uneven dirt floor which could not be called a basement even if we were polite.

To complete this picture, there was a leaning weather-beaten garage with cockeyed doors just north of the house. The whole ensemble had the character of a run-down, long-neglected pair of dog houses.

Okay. What did we want for $12,000, for crying out loud?

But, and this is the good part, it was on four of the most beautiful rolling acres, with a view of the Green Mountains and the Adirondacks, depending on which way you looked. We decided that was worth a good part of the $12,000, by Long Island standards anyway.

But the *best* part of all this was how dumb we were. For the better part of December and all of January (no, there is only one warm season

35

in Vermont: July) these two brave, creative, and once-upon-a-time smart city slickers drove 10 miles each way and every day except Saturday and Sunday to work on a house with no heat. We turned on the oven in the new electric stove. Period. Was this cockeyed optimism? Denial? ("It's not that cold. The sun is shining.") THIRTY-EIGHT DEGREES IN A HOUSE AT NOON WITH THE OVEN ON IS COLD! But, folks, we kept our coats on. And our hats. And our gloves. And two pairs of socks. And boots over those. F'gawdssakes, what more do you need? This gave new meaning to the word "layering" which was the fashion buzzword of the day. I guess we were hip by necessity.

By February we were ready to spend a month in Florida. Which is what we most certainly did. Found a crummy apartment in Cocoa Beach, Florida (which town was recommended to us by Mrs. Lounsbury of the Dog Team, whom I'll introduce to you later), complete with palmetto bugs (great big cockroaches to you city folk) right on the Atlantic Ocean in Satellite Beach. That's where we thawed out--and crunched palmetto bugs. I had a mouth covered with sun blisters by the time we left for home. Sporting those, along with the tans we treasured and which came with the blisters, we could prove we'd spent a month in Florida.

When we finally drove up our Lake Beebe driveway in March, it felt like January on Long Island. But now we could get the temperature all the way up to 50 degrees in Whiting's kitchen at noon with the oven on. So we took our gloves off. And one pair of socks.

Here's what we did in chronological order from November on, with a month off for thawing. Warren moved the oil burner to the cellar. We put up walls and made rooms and dry-walled and spackled and textured and painted and wall-papered and put down floors and stained floors and installed counters and created one bath up and a half bath down and put in a dishwasher and a trendy white hood over the white stove. We painted the outside brown, and I took pictures before and after, inside and out, and I can show them to you if you think it would add to your Vermont experience.

It took us just about a year in the cold and the heat and in between and we sold the whole thing for $39,000, which was a lot of money in those days, and more than $12,000 on any day.

LOVELY VERMONT FARMHOUSE, c. 1790, on Four Acres of Meadow, just minutes from town conveniences. Horse Barn, Broad View of Adirondacks and Green Mountains. Comfortable home includes Three Bedrooms, 1½ Baths, Hot Water Heat and Woodstove, plus a Dry Basement. A rare find at $45,000. — No. 5157 (Photo)

**The Four Rolling Acres facing the
Adirondacks to the West**

WHITING, Before and After

Dining Room

Going Up? Down?

Kitchen Kapers

YOU CAN'T GET THERE FROM HERE

HOW FAR IS FAR?

LAKE BEEBE WAS MILES FROM ANYWHERE. (Lake Beebe is also an entity. It's the house we built there and lived in and not the lake itself. The lake is "the lake." I've already introduced you to Whiting. Soon you'll find out about The Gulf, and BARN.) Lake Beebe (or LBB as it was fondly called in my bookkeeping notebooks) was 25 miles northwest of Rutland. Twenty miles south of Middlebury. Ten miles north of Castleton Corners. Six miles from the nearest general store in the winter. A little less in the summer. And 250 miles from Long Island.

This Long Island woman, who used to be able to shop at a supermarket a mile away from home, thought all those miles were unnecessary. And scary.

"Wanna go buy some food?" I asked Warren at least once a week. "We could do a wash, too."

Off we'd go. Ma and Pa Go Marketing. Whenever I drove by myself I wondered what I'd do if I got lost. Call home from a phone booth? What phone booth? Where? This was before cell phones, of course.

I look back on my Sissy-Scaredy-Fraidy-Cat days now and smile, remembering how it was before I became a Big Shot.

One day I wanted to go to Brandon—-10 miles away--in a hurry and Warren wasn't available. I girded my loins and started out by myself. Brandon was east, over that way, and I'll bet that dirt road will cut out a lotta miles! But once I was on it, when I thought it should go left it went right. The farmhouses got more scarce by the mile. I could feel my SSFC lurking in my belly. Around the next bend was a sweet covered bridge. Well, I certainly don't want to drive over *that!* What if it won't hold us? The car and me? Oh, Lord, where can I turn around? Before the bridge?

41

After the bridge? If it holds us? Will I ever see my kids again? WAR-
REN!

It would be some months before I ventured forth alone a second time.
When our friend Chick Ogg told me how to get Vermont Department of
Transportation maps, I knew that's what sissies need. When the maps
arrived, I folded them just like real maps——they'd come in the mail folded
in half--and I kept them neat with a rubber band on the seat beside me in the
car. I saw there were more sweet little dirt roads in Rutland County than
the other kind. Fortified with maps I'd numbered in order of importance,
I began to go out solo early in the morning on a day with a good weather
forecast. With practice I got there and back. It was thrilling. A notch in
my belt.

But for about a year after we'd gotten to Vermont, Ma and Pa went to
the market and even did the wash together. I remember watching an all-
alone customer in the laundromat taking care of her laundry——sorting it,
measuring detergent, putting the wash into the washer and then the dryer,
and then folding it neatly into a basket before heading out——and being
struck by her confidence. I must have been on to something and preparing
myself to fly solo.

When did I begin to feel silly? It doesn't matter. "Enough of this Ma
and Pa stuff. I'm going alone!"

I think Warren was disappointed. He wasn't going to be able to drive
the shopping cart in Grand Union any more unless he went by himself.

SNOW AND OTHER FALLING THINGS

IF YOU TOOK ALL THE SNOW from here to California and piled it as high as an elephant's eye, chances are you'd be in Vermont. I know other states have snow and plenty of it. But I've lived only on Long Island and in Vermont and I know whereof I speak as far as snow in Vermont is concerned.

I loved the first snowfall every year, usually in November. After being without it all summer, it was good to see that it still remembered what it had to do and how to do it.

When the new snow year started, Warren and I got in the car and drove as the flakes started to fall. I'd go, "Whee! Isn't this pretty!" And it was. After three hours I'd had it, once I remembered that we might not see the bare old brown ground again for another five, sometimes six months. Yes, one year there was a May snowfall. That was sobering.

And snow was sneaky. It doesn't make any noise when it's coming down. To wake up in the morning after a quiet night and be greeted by several feet of snow can be a terrible blow, especially if I had to go to Rutland or the store six miles down Route 30.

One spring comes to mind. It was a cloudy day and I was driving somewhere when I heard Tap Tap Tap on the roof of the car. What's that? RAIN! Loud rain! Beautiful solid rain! Such a welcome melody!

I will not bore you with the number of times either Warren or I tried driving up the snow-covered driveway and had to stop because we hadn't gunned the engine hard enough to get all the way up, only to slip back a few feet, ending tail first in the nearest snow bank on the edge of a gully. Or ending up in the gully itself and how does one get out of a gully? For some reason I'd rather forget, it probably involved a contraption known as a come-along which had to be hitched around a stout tree. I think. The

43

memory lapse is intentional. Pain is pain. And the pain of being dumb is especially painful. I told you we had our dumb moments.

I want to stop here and let you in on why I thought we were dumb. I have been blessed with 20/20 hindsight 25 years later, and I can look back at that driveway, plowed or not, and wouldn't it have been smarter if we had arranged to have a small cars-sized level area carved out at the bottom of the driveway so that we could park our cars there and then walk (trudge) up the hill? Of course. Dumb. Probably what pains me even more is that in all those years with winters in them we never thought of building a garage. Duh.

We seldom used the snow for fun, except to hurl snowballs at each other. We never went skiing. Every Saturday night, though, from 7:30 to 8:00 p.m., if we had no plans to go ballroom dancing, I watched a TV show about cross-country skiing. I can still hear the background music playing over and over (and over!) as accompaniment to the skiers gliding through the snow. I went to the library and took out books on the subject, and learned to cross-country ski—in my head.

One Christmas Warren and I planned to give each other cross-country skis.

"Why don't we walk through the woods and see how we like the scene before committing?" one of us asked.

We found the nearest snow-filled woods and started walking. After about a half hour we looked at each other.

"Eh," we agreed. End of story.

Twenty-five years later I'm snow-shoeing and loving it. I tried to cross-country ski, kept falling and trying to get up with the skis still on and laughing myself silly. I saw snow-shoes as another option. I look funny tramping along but it's great exercise and I haven't fallen so far.

(SKIS)

THERE'S NO LOST LIKE SNOW LOST

BOTH OUR KIDS HAVE a healthy respect for the ocean. From the time they were tots, our summer fun revolved around Jones Beach. They learned early how to deal with the waves, and although they had no fear, they had plenty of respect for the water they were getting into.

Chris and her future husband Grady visited us in Vermont the Christmas after we moved in. Grady had grown up in the state of Washington, and the ocean wasn't his love, but the outdoors was and still is second nature to him.

We were all invited to a New Years Eve party that year, and Grady asked a neighbor about a good hiking trail. Don Sondergeld suggested that he and Chris find the Lake Hortonia campgrounds and he gave them pretty explicit directions to the site from our house on Lake Beebe. Not on the main road but through the woods. ("When you get to the big old maple tree, bear left and continue . . ." —-you get the picture.)

Within an hour of their setting out bravely at noon, I spotted the first snowflake. Warren was watching the Rose Bowl game on TV and I was watching the snow. Around 3:30 it was looking like a pretty serious snowfall out there. Around 4:15 it began to get dark and there was no sign of our hikers. We called Don to find out how we could get into the Hortonia campgrounds from the main road. We started out in Harvey (I'll introduce you to our little Nash Rambler later) and drove north on Route 30, turning left at the old roadside stand as we'd been told. The dirt road had been plowed previously but now there was another six inches of new snow. Our snow tires carried us as far as the plow had gone but beyond that the snow was probably over a foot deep.

On the plowed road, Warren spotted shoe prints.

46

"There's Grady's hiking boots tread. They got to this point and then it looks as if they decided to go back the other way. Not a good sign."

Warren tried to move the car forward so that we could point the high beams into the woods. We hoped the kids could see the lights and be guided out to safety. But the car slid and did the old back-up-into-a-gully trick. I got out and there was no doubt in my mind that I could push the car up and out. When one's child is in danger, a mother's strength can be awesome, even when the child is 22. I was indeed awesome as Warren rocked and gunned that little car's engine. It worked. Warren jumped out and we began to yell and honk the horn. Silence.

"Chris! Grady!" The silence continued after the echo. Again the shouts, and finally from what seemed like miles away, we heard a faint and brave but squeaky, "Dad! Mom!"

They had seen the high beams and out they stumbled into the circle of light. They looked almost as scared as they did on the day they got married a few years later. We hugged them hard and they climbed into the back seat.

Chris said, "I learned a long time ago how to respect the ocean. Tonight I learned how to respect the snow. We felt so helpless!" Then a minute or two later in hardly enough time to catch her breath, she asked, "We can still go to the Brandon Inn for dinner, can't we?"

Neither rain nor snow nor dark of night . . . has ever stopped these Shibers from going out to eat, so what could we say but, "Sure."

On the drive back to the house, our cool friend Grady explained in great detail his plan in the event they hadn't been found.

"I was going to gather pine boughs and make a lean-to for us to spend the night in."

I had a plan of my own. Early the next morning I went outside and gathered pine boughs for Grady's breakfast.

Harvey resting in the driveway

THE BENNY

WE WERE INTRODUCED TO Franklin stoves when we spent a week each summer in a rustic cabin at a fishing camp in the Belgrade Lakes region of Maine way before we found Vermont. The stove sat against the back wall of the small main room so that its heat could spread through the bedrooms, too. Warren began to call it The Benny. You know. Benny Franklin, the Benjamin who invented this efficient wood-burning stove.

When we were thinking about a woodstove for Lake Beebe we knew it had to be a Benny. Now that I'm back on Long Island, one of the things I miss most is the smell of a fire in a woodstove.

The heat in our little Vermont house was electric, and even though it's inexpensive to install, the electric bills for that kind of heat can be exorbitant and scary. Whenever I walked past the Central Vermont Public Service (CVPS was the endearing acronym) meter on the side of the house, I could see that little wheel a-turning and hear that little wheel a-whizzing. That's why we burned eight-and-a-half cords of wood each year.

The wood for the stove. Ah! That operation took up a lot of time. We never had to be bored because whenever we ran out of things to do, we remembered The Benny and its needs.

First, Warren had to fell the trees. And not just any old tree: hardwood, like maple. Not pine or birch or spruce or aspen, which we had in abundance. They're too soft. And if you had to burn pine, you could be sure that creosote would line the stovepipe in no time and eventually you'd have a flue fire and be scared out of your wits. We had several and we were. We tried to stick to the maple.

Then with his trusty chain saw Warren had to cut the trunk in log-length segments and cart them over to the upended stump on which he had to split the segment into Benny-width logs. (Are you still with me? Good. Then you can help me haul those logs onto the deck at the front and sides of the house.) I used a wheelbarrow for the hauling task and that was before I was into upper-body strength training. (Now I use weights.) When I remembered, I stacked those logs three one way and three the opposite way. When I forgot, I just stacked them neatly in a row, but they dried out better the other way.

Now it is good to know right here that all of this should be done by the month of March *before the winter* which follows the fall of that same year. <u>*The March before.*</u> But not being wise to the ways of Vermont, these two Long Islanders were still trying to keep the home fires burning with logs from trees that had been felled during the spring and summer just before we were scheduled to burn them. (I'm lying. Some years it was just two weeks.) As a result, *our* wood was never seasoned properly, forsooth. And the bloody logs spit and hissed from all the moisture still remaining in them. The fire still smelled good, but we had definitely failed Trees for Burning in Woodstoves.

Right after we moved in, Warren, who was clever in the creativity department, made a log-holding wheel from a long link of heavy chain which he'd welded into a three-foot in diameter holder. I remember (and this was around the time of Charles Schulz's book "*Happiness Is . . .")* telling someone that Happiness Is a Wheel Full of Logs.

Every August in Vermont there comes a spell cool enough to tell us fall is on its way, and after a couple of years of bringing The Benny back to life after the summer's warm weather, I looked forward to that spell when the August morning temperature would lower itself to just around 40 outside. It was time to light The Benny!

That's when I knew why Vermonters tend to be tough Yankees. They know that winter's always just around the corner, and they know they can make it through another one by dint of their smarts, their industry, the seat of their pants and their woodstoves, whose logs most of them have had ready for over a year.

Good hardy folk. I never met a Vermonter who was a sissy. Winter didn't scare them. Not much of anything else did either.

Yes, I miss that smell of wood burning. And I miss The Benny. Come to think of it, I miss those tough old Vermonters as well. I miss Warren, too. Of course, Warren.

DESCRIBE A CIRCULAR STAIRCASE (WITHOUT USING YOUR HAND)

"WELL, I GUESS IF WE'RE GOING TO STAY here a while we should probably make more room," Warren said and I agreed.

"Let's figure out what we need."

As soon as we had a moment to spare, we went sideways and up on the side of the existing house. We would get rid of the two bedrooms across the back and use that space for living area, leaving one bedroom for the king and queen downstairs and creating two bedrooms upstairs in the addition. A half bath would be added up there, and the space underneath became a sitting room/bedroom/my office/you-name-it.

We knew we'd need the addition only rarely in the winter for our kids' visits and for our hardy friends who liked snow, so we cleverly closed it off with a six-foot triple-glazed patio door. This kept The Benny's heat where we wanted it when we were alone, besides giving the living area the illusion of space. It worked.

The kitchen door became a window, adding needed wall space beneath it in the form of a peg board for utensils and useless but handsome accessories.

Now the question: how do we get upstairs without using too much space for stairs. Ah, John Joy of the Dog Team Restaurant had mentioned a circular staircase he didn't need any more. Wonder how much he wants for it.

We drove up to Middlebury to see him and made a deal with no hassle, as I recall. We had it delivered in pieces and then had to figure out how to assemble it so that the bottom step would be gracefully accessible and the

52

top step wouldn't land us facing a wall. Warren figured it out, of course. It would have taken me much longer.

It looked so grand once it was in place that Warren said it needed a skylight above it to further dramatize it. He cut a hole in the roof, inserted a domed skylight, and that bit of light was just the ticket to add the necessary illumination for anyone to go up or down during the day and even at night when there was a full moon.

We put in some more ever-lovin' electric radiators and called as many friends as we could think of to come up and see us sometime.

Now we could entertain right around the calendar if we wanted to, and more and more we wanted to.

Lake Beebe. Warren Starting Phase Two.

Lake Beebe. Phase Two Finished.

THE BATTLEFIELD ROAD

'OH, LET'S GO BACK BY the Battlefield Road!"

There are two ways to get to and from Lake Beebe and Castleton. One is by way of Route 30, the two-lane paved road you've already met, and the Battlefield Road, which is just dirt and ruts most of the way. The latter one is longer but more scenic, if you favor a Revolutionary field-of-battle scene, and the smaller scene of the weary old cemetery next to it, complete with leaning headstones and restless ghosts. There's a sprinkling of farmhouses along the way, and the road loops and winds and rises and falls on what seems like an endless journey from Route 4 to Route 30. Very few people take the Battlefield Road unless they live there or want to be alone. Very alone.

Movies are a passion of mine, but I hadn't seen any since our move some months earlier. The theaters were only in Rutland and Middlebury——one in each——both 20 to 25 mile trips in either direction. By the time summer of 1975 rolled around, I had a big hunger. There was a drive-in on Route 4 in Castleton, probably the last in existence in Vermont, and did we care what was playing? *The Exorcist* and we hadn't seen it.

We both sank down in the front seat of the car during the head-spinning scene. We put our hands in front of our faces, something we hadn't had to do since *Psycho.* The vomiting was pretty scary, too, but we were able to get through that sitting up straight and peeking through our fingers.

We left the drive-in after midnight when I had the bright idea to take the Battlefield Road home. It was a beautiful clear night but no moon. Within a mile we both knew we had chosen the wrong time to try an unfamiliar route. Most of Vermont had gone to bed. It was very dark and we had just survived *The Exorcist.*

"What's that?" I asked suddenly.

"Oh, that must be the battlefield."

55

"Oh, gosh! What's THAT?"

"That's gotta be the cemetery."

I could hardly make out the headstones in the dark but I was now watching ghosts floating around.

"I'm scared. Are you?"

Warren then said out loud what we were both too frightened to say.

"Wouldn't it be awful if we got a flat out here?"

The occasional houses were pitch dark. Now I could hear the sound of eerie hollow laughter as we bumped along. Warren was trying to avoid the ruts but we couldn't go fast enough to stay ahead of our fear. When I heard the high hissing voices in front of us alternating with the deep guttural moans coming from behind, I slid down on my haunches, put my hands over my face and didn't look through my fingers until I felt the smooth surface of Route 30 at last.

Good old Harvey (Warren had named our little white car Harvey because when it just sat there on its wheels it seemed to be the same size as Elwood P. Dowd's big white rabbit standing up) got us home safely. When we got to the top of the driveway, we both sighed in unison, "We made it!"

The next morning when Warren stepped outside to check the oil in the car, he came right back in.

"Guess what?" he said. "Harvey's got a flat."

Elaine Polson Shiber

ONE POTATO, TWO POTATO

WHEN I LIVED ON LONG ISLAND, I never, no never, drove out in June to the end of the island to pick strawberries or anything else. Many of my friends did but I didn't. Why drive over 50 miles to pick something you can buy at a supermarket a mile away?

Vermont changed all that, at least where potatoes and apples were concerned. Joan and Bob, my sister and her husband, visited us from New Jersey one weekend. While I was looking through the *Rutland Herald* because I was going to take a nap if I didn't, I spotted an ad for PICK YOUR OWN POTATOES! Neat idea! Joan and I said, "Why not?" The ad had the directions to the farm which was not too far away and now we could find out first hand how potatoes grow.

Off we went in Harvey, our swell Nash Rambler, to pick potatoes. We found the farm and saw all those rows of potatoes the farmer had taken his plow to (we guessed) and the potatoes were lying around just ripe for the plucking. We'd brought Grand Union bags and started to fill them. Full. I'm sure we had no plans for what we would do with all those potatoes but what did it matter? This was *fun!*

We finally had enough potatoes to last at least a year. Just think: potato salad, fried potatoes, mashed potatoes, ham and potatoes au gratin, peanut butter and potatoes, potatoes on the half shell, potatoes Stroganoff, potatoes St. Jacques. And how about potato soup? Baked? Plain old boiled with a little butter and dill weed? Oh, the list was endless!

We could leave now. I got no farther than 20 yards when suddenly Harvey's wheels sank slowly into some mud that hadn't been there before as far as I knew. I got out to survey the situation and Joan moved over behind the wheel because she was older and always wanted to be boss. Joan would get us out! Hooray, Joan! She gunned the engine and got into the mud just a little deeper. So she gunned again.

I yelled, "Joan, let's reconnoiter," and I still don't know where *that* came from. So I reconnoitered. Joan, however, wanted no part of reconnoitering and gunned again and again. Suddenly who should appear but the farmer and his small son. Dad was driving a tractor and stopped near enough to watch what these babes with the funny car were doing. His son jumped off the tractor and came over to watch us, too. Joan gunned again, spewing potato mud all over the place. Dad yelled, "Watch out, Duane! She's car-razy!" But Joan finally got it right by gunning and backing up and easing that little Harvey right out of the muck. I jumped in then because my reconnoitering job was finished.

We stopped at the farmhouse on the way out and paid for what we had picked up. I'm sure it was pittance, and we weren't asked to pay for the damage to the field. They were probably just glad to see us go.

When we showed Warren and Bob the fruits-—or vegetables-—of our labor, they both said, "Great!" And then, "But why so many?"

BENJIE

REMEMBER WHITING? That house/entity almost to Middlebury? The old/new farmhouse? On the west side of the two-lane highway known as Route 30 on a little over four acres? (Oh yeah. *That* farmhouse.)

We had almost finished the renovation and it was about ready for occupancy. So we occupied it for two weeks anyway while we rented our lake house to a family from Long Island.

One summer evening as we were cleaning up after dinner, we heard a small but insistent knock on the kitchen door leading from the front yard. Framed in the doorway on the other side of the screen stood a husky blond boy of about six or seven. We opened the door for him. We invited him into the kitchen, and when I put my hand on his shoulder I could feel that he was trembling.

"Mister, can you help me get my cow? She got loose and the bull is gonna knock his door down to get to her and the babysitter is on the phone and she can't help me. Can you?"

He told us his name was Benjie. His cow's name? Mona.

"Where do you live?"

"That house right up the road." He pointed a shaky finger.

Warren said, "Okay, let's find your cow. I'll get some rope."

By now Benjie's lower lip was quivering. Warren followed him in the direction Benjie thought the cow had wandered. I stayed in the yard awaiting word from the men because Warren had ordered me to "Wait here!"

In fewer than 10 minutes, Warren, holding one end of a rope, rounded the corner of the house, followed by Mona on the other end, followed by Benjie, who was grinning now. Every time the cow yanked on her end of the rope, Warren's head flew back. He looked funny but I tried not to laugh. And Mona wasn't the little pet calf I had expected to see. Mona was almost full-grown and a lovely brown and white color. Just like a real cow. I'd never been this close to a cow before and I could feel intimidation setting in.

Now it was time for my orders.

"Elaine, I want you to get the car and bring it over here. We're going to tow Mona back home and you can drive!" (Who, me?—-drive a cow home?)

The three of them—-Warren, Benjie and Mona—-walked out into the middle of Route 30, and while Warren made HALT! gestures with his head to the line of cars beginning to collect on the road, I quickly backed the car out of the driveway into the middle of the two lanes and maneuvered it into towing position just ahead of the Band of Three. It was getting dark by now. The rope was finally secured to the bumper, and while Warren and Benjie tried to guide Mona forward as she meandered from road-edge to road-edge as far as the rope would allow, I tugged Mona behind the car, my head and the car jerking with Mona's every pause. I decided not to laugh *then* either.

As this ragtag gang moved steadily onward, I began to see the drama being enacted: two-lane road in the middle of Vermont farm country, Long Island woman driving funny little white car, stout rope, brown and white cow, tall bearded man, small brave boy, six assorted cars with lights on following slowly behind and not honking—and I thought, "If my friends could see me now . . . "

I'll bet by the next day Benjie had forgotten all about it.

I'll bet Warren and I didn't and look who's writing about it now.

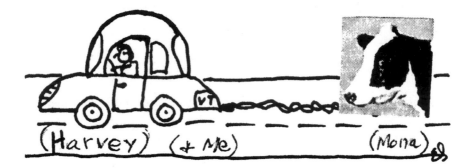

(Harvey) (+ Me) (Mona)

WILLY WOO

SOMEWHERE DURING THOSE FEW YEARS when I was trying to figure out what I wanted to do when I grew up, I was asked by some local kennel owners if I would oversee the animals in their care while they were away at a dog show one weekend. They were going to pay me, so why not? And Warren had agreed to spend Saturday night with me as an overnight guest.

The kennel was a well-run, well-cared-for and clean enterprise. The animal smells had been kept to a minimum, and I walked through the main room looking into the neat and tidy cages as I went. Big dogs. Little dogs. Cats were kept in a separate room and I looked them over, too. I didn't spend too much time with the cats on my first walk-through. Either cats are aloof creatures or they just didn't like my looks because not a one of those four or five cats even gave me a tumble. I like dogs better. Their tails wag just for the heck of it.

The owners had told me each animal's name so that if a customer came in for his animal he wouldn't suspect that I was a novice. I had been given a list of which dogs to feed in the morning and the food amounts. Some of the bigger dogs had to be fed at night as well, and I was pleased that I could keep all of this straight. I also opened the doors to their own private runs, figuring out how to get them in again later. Food.

I've always had a strange relationship with dogs. I don't like *all* dogs. There are a few dogs whose personalities I love and gravitate toward. We seem to connect and they edge their way into my heart. Just like kids. Some I like and some I don't.

I spotted Willy Woo as a favorite. Maybe it was his name. He was a skinny, wiry little thing, about 10 inches tall and he was black with a few random white markings. He was not synchronized in the markings department which made him even more appealing. We were not dealing

63

with an AKC purebred here. Willy Woo was probably a terrier of some kind, but what did I know? I only knew I liked him immediately. And I think the feeling was mutual. When he wagged his tail in greeting, the action went right up to his skinny little head, and was that a smile playing around his skinny little mouth?

Saturday night I fed those dogs who got two meals a day, cleaned out any deposits left for me, made sure each dog had a filled water bowl and said, "Goodnight, all you darlings!" I turned out most of the lights and went into the house to prepare dinner and then finally went to sleep.

Sunday morning, I headed out early for the kennel, heard the familiar barks, opened the door and slowly made my way along the cages to check on my charges.

"Oh, Lord. Willy Woo!" That sweet skinny animal was lying on his back with his four little legs sticking straight up in the air.

"He died! Oh, Lord! *WARREN!*" He came running into the kennel and confirmed my diagnosis.

Oh, what to do? What to do?

"We're going to have to call Eddie and Jane and tell them, aren't we? But we don't have a number at the show! And even if we could call them, what could they do until they get home? But if they don't find out until they get home, won't there be hell to pay? Boy, is this a mess!"

"Did I kill him? How could I have killed him? Of all the dogs to die! My favorite! I feel terrible!"

We were standing in the owners' kitchen and we agreed that there was nothing we could do then except cover that little body until Eddie and Jane and the owners were told.

But I was feeling so guilty. Guilty and sad. I'd been given a responsibility and I had failed. I'd failed dog-sitting.

We walked slowly out to the kennel to the sound of barking dogs and proceeded to Willy Woo's cage. And who was standing up on all fours, wagging his skinny tail right up to his little head? His Majesty Willy Woo himself. We almost cried with relief.

We never shared with the kennel owners what we thought had happened that Sunday.

And I never dog-sat again.

SERENDIPITY

SERENDIPITY IS DEFINED in my dictionary as "the faculty of happening upon fortunate discoveries when not in search of them." I like to say that it's finding an unexpected treasure when you're busy looking for something else. I was looking for sanity and discovered my love of the real estate business.

While Warren and I were reinventing Whiting, a man stopped frequently to check on our progress. Fred lived about three miles north of our renovated house, off Route 30, and he sold real estate.

Our original plan was to open a restaurant in the house after it was finished. We were even thinking of names, with the help of friends: North 40, A Different Drummer. We thought they were clever, each and every one. Warren was to be the chef because he loved to cook, and I'd be the hostess and take all those calls for all those reservations as they poured in. I'd also greet all those customers who would also be pouring in, and wait on tables if I had to.

Then we met a couple of *bona fide* restaurateurs, Chick and Maris Ogg, who invited us to their home for dinner and told us all about OSHA and food preparation and laws governing restaurant ownership in Vermont, and things like that. When Warren dragged me home from their lovely and informational dinner party, I had the worst headache I'd ever experienced. The next day we abandoned our original plan.

Okay, if it's not going to be a restaurant, what are we going to do with this house? Why, sell it, of course.

This is where Fred comes into the story. When the house was near completion, he estimated the price we could probably get for it. He invited us for coffee at his home one morning and we met his wife, too. While we all sat around their kitchen table, I asked, "How do you become a real estate salesman?" What I heard was silence but what I saw was a red flag going up.

"Oh, you don't want to do that!" chirped Blanche. (I hadn't said I wanted "to do that." I just wanted to know how one went about doing "that," but they must have guessed I was up to no good.)

"Fred tells me you're wonderful at interior design! Right, Fred?"

"Right! She is!" Fred agreed with enthusiasm.

The groundwork had been laid. If there was anything this Long Island woman could understand and sink her teeth into it was competition. I was ready! Now I would find out for myself how to become a real estate salesperson in Vermont because *these* folks certainly weren't going to tell me. Did they want me messing around in that business? No way!

I talked to June Sherline, who'd become a good friend and my mentor in the world of business in particular, and life in Vermont (and everywhere else) in general.

First I'd need a sponsor, someone already in the business.

"Let me talk to Ida Young. She'll sponsor you and you'll learn a lot from her." Ida Young did and I did. Then I signed up for a 10-week real estate course with broker Olga Cassella in Rutland and I drove into town one night a week. I had a book and I studied and studied. All summer long I studied. Real estate was becoming my new passion.

As it turned out, this was a good match for me. I like houses—floor plans, traffic flow, lighting and decorating--and I could use my people skills. I'd been told by a career counselor on Long Island that I had "people skills," and when I asked her what she meant she said, "You're comfortable meeting new people, you seem to have the ability to make friends, and you understand group dynamics." Hmmm. People skills, and now I could use them here in Vermont.

My first hurdle after doing all that studying was to take the sales exam, scheduled for a day in September. The weekend before, I took a crash course with John Faraci, another real estate broker in Rutland, and my brain was filled with deeds and amortization and eminent domain and Vermont rules and regulations. I loved all that stuff! (In my next life, I want to be a lawyer.)

At that time the Vermont Real Estate Commission gave only four exams a year: two sales and two brokers. Then two years of apprenticeship as a salesperson was required before you could take the brokers exam. (All memory details are approximate.) The rate of exam failure was very high. Sometimes only 50% of the candidates passed, and when I took it no calculators were allowed on all those numbers! Pencils and paper only.

My neighbor and friend Ruth Ebbesen kindly offered to drive me the two hours or more to Montpelier so that I could start the four-hour test at 8:00 a.m. in good condition. While I was in the auditorium taking the test, Ruth waited around town so that she could drive me home again. Walking back to her car, I was so full of exam questions and my answers that I felt uncertain as to whether I'd passed or not. Comparing notes with others later left me just as unsure.

Several weeks had to go by before I knew the results. Each afternoon I rode my bike out to our mailbox on Route 30. One day there it was: Vermont Real Estate Commission on the top left corner of the envelope. I passed! I rang the bell on the handlebar all the way back to the house and Warren ran down the driveway to meet me. Imagine! A 50-year-old woman had taken an ETS/Princeton exam and passed! On my first try! Wow!

Maris and Chick Ogg surprised us with a bottle of champagne that night and we polished it off. I even took a picture, of course.

I'd learned all about "real estate." Now all I had to do was learn the business. That took a few years.

* * *

This is a good time to compare my Vermont real estate training and experience with my New York venture into real estate later. Even though there was no reciprocity between the two states, when I came back to Long Island I considered returning to that passion of mine and checked out requirements, etc.

I found a real estate agency that seemed right for me, took the very easy sales exam in about a half hour, and spent a few months part-time getting acquainted with the business here.

Without knocking my now home state of New York, the difference between the two states regarding real estate was considerable. I found that the Vermont Real Estate Commission was a group of professionals, and that the majority of brokers and salespeople I worked with dealt fairly and honestly with the public and with me. On those rare occasions when one would slip, he or she was called before the commission.

I must confess that after trying to become a real estate agent here in New York, it became apparent to me that I didn't have the guts or the stomach for it.

FREEZING RAIN IS NOT SLEET

I NEVER SAW FREEZING RAIN until I lived in Vermont. Sleet I knew. It fell on Long Island every now and then. But freezing rain doesn't freeze until it hits a surface, like the ground, or a car, whereas sleet comes out of the sky already frozen. Hail? I know hailstones can fall any season of the year but hail's not in the same league as sleet or freezing rain. Ask any meteorologist. And if you're already a meteorologist, you'd better call me if I need straightening out.

I'd made plans to fly to California to visit Chris and Grady one February morning, and the weather forecast the day before was for snow the next day——not a fortuitous omen. We kept listening to the radio and it never got any better, but no worse either.

Warren finally expressed the worry he was having about my getting to the plane out of Albany-—a two-hour drive from Hubbardton——the next morning. He suggested we leave that afternoon, get a jump on the weather, stay in a motel at the Albany airport and I'd be all set for the flight to California when it took off. Thanks, Warren! Let's go!

It was snowing just lightly when we left home, but by the time we got to the New York State Thruway 45 minutes away, the snow was turning to what we thought was rain. Our windshield wipers were shuttling back and forth, and then there appeared on the road a NYS snow plow, and it was throwing sand in our path. "Hmmm. What's that for?" we asked out loud, for we were not wise to the ways of way-up-north weather. As the wiper blades started pushing something other than water back and forth we were still puzzled and still not so wise.

We found the motel at which we'd made reservations and pulled into their covered-over entrance to the registration desk. When Warren got back into the car, we headed for the spot where we could park just outside our room.

Whoops! I couldn't stand because if I did I would fall down. The car was covered with ice and so was the walkway on which we could approach our room. What to do? Wait until it melted? That was definitely an option.

Luckily I remembered how to crawl on my hands and knees from when I was about 11 months old. And that's what I did. Warren would rather have eaten worms than been seen crawling on his hands and knees by the millions of people who had now of course gathered around watching, and so he fell not so gracefully twice before getting to the door I had unlocked and had opened while I was hanging on to the doorknob for dear life.

The next morning the weather forecast proved to have been wrong and the sun was shining. I had no trouble getting to the plane and taking off for California.

California was nice. I saw lots of flowers by the side of the road. All this and it was February--in California and Vermont.

HUBBARDTON GULF

RIGHT AROUND THAT TIME——it was 1978——three things happened: One, we had a few extra bucks in our jeans; two, we needed another challenging project to worry about, and the third thing was seeing that sign on Route 30 about a mile from home.

HOUSE FOR SALE. The house was vacant but there was a phone number penciled in. I called the number and a man told me everything I wanted to know: $16,000, house needed work, and it sat on eight acres, most of which ran south of the house along Route 30.

When I called the bank in Rutland to find out the mortgage interest rates of the day I found out that 10% was just about right. We also had found out that the owner held an existing mortgage of 7-1/2% which sounded more interesting, if you'll pardon the pun.

Warren was willing to get a bank mortgage, and I thought, naaah, not if we can take over the existing mortgage. My real estate knowledge was paying off.

"Warren, let's (you) call the owners to see if they want a nice down payment and a nice check each month from a nice mature couple."

Warren did and the owners finally did, too, with a little persuasion. I'm not sure if the Artful Persuader was Warren with the owners, or me with Warren.

The young couple had never lived in the house. They had bought it for speculation and hadn't started to improve it. We set out to improve it because we were getting good at it, in all kinds of weather, including December and January. But this house had a well-functioning oil burner in the basement and a hot water heater which could furnish us with lots of hot water for cleaning.

The bright kitchen, dining room, and living room were neat and welcoming, and there was a small bedroom and a bathroom on the first floor, too. We could see the possibilities because we were still developing the vision thing with which we'd both been blessed. Upstairs had two ample bedrooms, and room for another full bath. The bath on the first floor had a fine old tub on a platform (no, no claw feet-—that was from another era) that had charm, a frosted glass window, and a toilet that was pleading for a quick death. The sink also had a touch of charm about it and could stay or join the toilet if we chose.

The house sat between two good-sized hills (mountains, if you insist) and when the sun was shining, it was available for viewing on the south side of the house from about 10 in the morning until almost three in the afternoon. Lots of windows on the south, and 25 years later I'm still feeling that warmth and delight from those five hours each sunny winter day. As I'm writing this, I'm aware that I fell in love with every house we built or worked on in Vermont.

Warren and I duplicated our Whiting efforts, and this time he laid a slate floor in the kitchen and built his own brand of cabinets above the new yellow linen-look counters. We added a new stove, refrigerator and sink, and he put in the sweetest window next to the door to replace the old one. Of course, a Benny was added to the far corner of the living room near the stairs going up and down. He also added an eight-foot-wide deck with built-in benches along the south side of the house-—that was so handy for resting packages from the supermarket on while I got out my keys-—added flood lights to guide our steps at night, and I can still remember watching the falling snow by the light of those floods as I sat at the dining room table some nights before going upstairs to bed. There was an existing enclosed porch across the front of the house facing the road. We ignored that until we dolled it up for my office one summer. My real estate sign was placed next to the road right away, though, the better to find me, my dears.

The Hubbardton Gulf house became our first rental property, and our first tenants was a group of Castleton college boys who rented the house for part of one semester. When they were leaving, I made an inspection of the inside, and found that the boys had split some logs for Benny-burning on the carpet (ouch!) and had left spaghetti-sauce spotted pots, dishes, plates, silverware and kitchen floor untouched. They almost cried when they asked for their security deposit back, and I said, "Sorry, kids, that's not even negotiable." That's when I learned that there's a not-so-fine line between being a good-hearted schnook and being a patsy. Rental properties are a business. I learned the hard way, but I learned.

Warren and I spent a few happy and accessible winters there whenever the house was vacant and available. Warren would rather have stayed at the lake every winter, but trying to get up that driveway wasn't the thrilling challenge for me that it was for him, so we compromised and stayed at the Gulf.

You haven't asked me why that section of Route 30 was known as the Hubbardton Gulf. Well, it was a gulf because there was a stream running alongside the road, with hills/mountains on either side, but the best part is that now it is so designated because of Don Sondergeld, one of the vacation homeowners on the west side of Lake Beebe. Don contacted the state, and, if I know him at all, he said to the state, "Now, listen here . . ." And after letters were written back and forth for several months, not only is Hubbardton Gulf so written on every Vermont map worth its salt, but there are now two green state signs proclaiming HUBBARDTON GULF at each end of the gulf on Route 30.

HUBBARDTON GULF, Before and After

REAL ESTATE. PART II

UNTIL I GOT MY REAL ESTATE ACT together by passing the brokers exam, I found I was happy using my talents helping Warren build houses. I also dabbled in real estate as a salesperson. I say "dabbled" because my heart wasn't in it: I had trouble staying the course and I wasn't focused. But because I was a member of the Rutland County Board of Realtors, I had to drive into Rutland each Tuesday morning at 9:30 for the Multiple Listing Service business meeting.

Ida Young, the broker for whom I was working, lived in Rutland and after the meeting I went to her office in her home and kept her MLS notebook up to date with my new pages. I didn't really know what I was doing but it seemed to be the right thing and maybe I'd learn something. If the phone rang I could answer it because Ida wasn't there and I could play office, which was really what it felt like—-"make-believe."

But I started to feel useful and was finally seeing what this business was all about. Now I understand that the best thing happening to me each week was that I was meeting all kinds of lively, fascinating brokers and salespeople who worked in the area. They definitely knew what *they* were doing and I watched, listened and learned.

When I decided to go for broker (sorry, but I had to say it) and began to study like mad, I saw some possibilities for my life as I became immersed in a subject that I'd discovered on my own and was seeing where it could take me, at least where work was concerned. I was growing up without my noticing it or even trying, but I could now see the value in autonomy! Warren and I were working well together—-the rocks in my head fit the holes in his, as my friend Joyce Houston once said—-and we each had our own areas of expertise which helped us to avoid the inevitable conflicts. Most of the time we weren't competing—-oh, we had our moments of toe-to-toe contests-—and I think that's good in a marriage. But much of my time in the late seventies was spent helping Warren do his thing while I was adjusting to my new wooded existence and experiencing waves of homesickness when I let them in. I'm told I looked pretty good but I think I was just a little nuts at least some of the time.

I look back on those years and see how much I depended on Warren (and I was lucky he was dependable), but when I could let go of that and fly solo once in a while, my independence/autonomy was something he supported (lucky there, too) and it felt so darned good to me! What's that healthy arrangement in a relationship? Inter-dependent? That's what we were becoming.

While I prepared for the test, I discovered that I loved math. (The brokers exam is *really* filled with math.) In high school I squeaked through my algebra and geometry NYS regents exams. I'd fallen into the trap of "girls don't do well in math," that popular myth when I was growing up. The practice exams were filled with geometry and capitalization and wonderful problems like that and my mouth began to water. That winter when Warren and I went to Florida to thaw out, my brother-in-law Bob and I spent many a happy hour doing math! When we came home, I took another weekend crash course, and then passed the exam. This time, though, I drove to Montpelier by myself and bedded down in a motel so that I would be ready to take the exam early the next morning. That was definitely the grown-up thing to do, and wasn't *I* becoming the non-sissy at last!

A few months later I went to work as an independent contractor at The Riley Agency, a real estate office in Castleton. It was good to be back working with people every day, and I made a few healthy bucks besides. One morning, as I bounced out of bed to go to a closing, I thought, "They're gonna pay me today for what I know!" I'd never felt that way in my life.

The next summer I had my own agency with my own classy custom-made sign by the side of the road in the Hubbardton Gulf. My daughter

Carole designed smart-looking business cards and stationery for me. Warren and I scraped and painted and dolled up the neglected enclosed front porch and that was my office. I added a door for a desk, some file cabinets, a couple of white wicker chairs, a lamp or two, wall hangings and a couple of spiffy throw rugs to liven up the place. Even threw a few outdated magazines on the table in case any clients or customers had to wait.

Spring, summer and fall were filled with buyers and sellers and weekly advertising and closings, and in the winter and now and then during the rest of the year I was working with Warren and thawing out in Florida. Tom Degnen, a fine young salesman, was working with me. I made many friends and I was having such a good time!

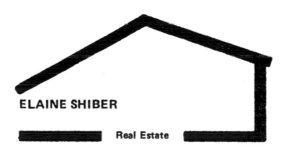

ELAINE SHIBER

Real Estate

Route 30, Hubbardton, Bomoseen, VT 05732
(802) 273-2994

CRITTERS, VARMINTS AND BUGS. OH, MY!

I JUST WASN'T USED to creepy-crawlies, that's all. Long Island had crickets, house flies and horse flies, lady bugs, Japanese beetles, mosquitoes and crabs--horseshoe and the plain ole garden variety kind.

Vermont was another matter. While we lived there, I had to get used to big black carpenter ants, woodchucks, field mice, raccoons, bats, chipmunks, a lot of daddy long legs, snakes, chameleons, porcupines, eels, dragonflies, beavers as well as the usual assortment of spiders, flies, and, of course, mosquitoes. Rumor had it there were bears and cougars, too, but it couldn't be proved by us.

I never thought I'd be able to co-exist with any of these creatures. Lucky for me, though, I found that after a while familiarity not only breeds contempt, it can also breed, well, familiarity.

The carpenter ants were fun. When we first arrived at the lake from Long Island for a short visit before we moved there, we found the big black ants had moved in. I loved watching those big guys march across the table and then fall kerplunk! on the floor below without a pause. Then I could step on them. I got to love the crunch. Ant traps then became part of the decor.

A daddy long legs traveled with me one day on the floor of the passenger side of the car and was making its way toward me, one leg at a time. I had to stop, place a map under it gently (those legs are fragile) and deposit him on the side of the road. My skin was crawling. I had squashed one of these sweet harmless friends once before I knew they were on our side. I still haven't gotten over it. I hope the one I dropped off lived a long and happy life.

I even learned how to cover a friendly bug with a paper cup, slide a piece of cardboard under it, open the door with my third hand and set it free. I was getting so brave. So sweet.

The mosquito season arrived right after the mud season, when the weather finally became outdoorsy and inviting. We had to stay in for two more weeks. The mosquitoes were usually gone by the Fifth of July. Then the deer flies came to fill in the gap. We did the Deer-Fly-Arm-Circle-Swing on our walks, day and night, unless we were smart enough to remember to wear hats.

RACCOONS

As everyone knows, raccoons love garbage. We don't but they do. Each night those raccoon rascals were able, with their dexterous hands (paws?), to open one or two of the pails we had placed on the deck for our leftovers. We finally won because our brains were bigger.

All I knew about raccoons I'd learned from cartoons: that sweet face with that sweet mask. I decided to see one face-to-mask one night. I got out of bed at the first sound of banging and turned on the deck light. All I caught was the raccoon's big rump following its sweet mask over the edge of the deck. And I said, even though I knew he couldn't speak English, "Oh, you're not so cute. I thought you were cute but you're NOT. You're a big fat faker with a sweet mask, pretty hands (paws?) and a blowzy body you should be ashamed of. Get some exercise, Fatso. AND STOP OPENING OUR GARBAGE CANS!"

We went to Gilmore's, our local lumber yard, and bought those clever locks that fit on garbage lids that even *I* couldn't figure out how to work.

BEEBE BATS

That's the name we gave to the nervous objects swooping around the lake at dusk. Those of you over 40 will recognize that moniker, and the rest of you will have to check with one of your elders.

My first serious bat contest took place when my sister Joan and her husband Bob were visiting us. Warren wasn't home, and I had brought a few dried clothes into the house from the clothesline. That's how the bat must have gotten in. He was sleeping in a clean shirt.

Suddenly all hell broke loose. Joan started screaming.

"A bat! A bat! It's rabid! We'll be bitten! Get it out of here!"

The bat continued to swoop and scare, but if he was as blind as a bat, he was a blind bat and flying by radar. Small comfort. Bob ran around looking for a broom.

In times of crisis, especially if someone is hysterical (and Joan had that wide-eyed hysterical look) I remain composed. In control. Level-headed. (Remember "reconnoiter?") One must remain calm at all cost. I've seen movies where the hero must slap the overwrought one across the face—-whoomp whoomp bang--to bring the other to his senses. I was tempted but was too composed (and too cowed, if you must know) to slap my big sister. I grabbed the broom and swung it wildly to show the bat the door Bob had managed to open. Out it went. We sat down and caught our collective breath. Joan was still wild-eyed but she'd stopped screaming.

The next time we had a bat experience, both Joan and I remained calm.

Diane, the tenant in the BARN, about which I'll tell you later, called to tell us there was a bat in her house. Joan was so composed in our house a mile away that she suggested I let Diane deal with it herself, but Joan hadn't heard about the first rule when you have a good tenant: Keep 'er happy. I liked Diane, and knew she wasn't wimpish. Her cat had dropped the bat at Diane's feet as a gift. The bat had been playing dead but was now doing his swooping best to scare the bejeebers out of his host.

I grabbed the Bat-broom and Joan and I tiptoed into Diane's house. (Why did we tiptoe? Who wasn't supposed to hear us? The bat? The cat? Diane?) I repeated my Beebe Bat performance to thunderous applause from the cat. Joan didn't scream this time but just issued commands while Diane hid bravely behind the couch. The bat finally found the open door and we haven't seen it since.

THE PORCUPINE AND THE WHITE HUNTER

"What's that noise?" Something had awakened us and then we heard those intermittent scratching sounds. It was 3:12 a.m. by the digital clock. Warren said it must be a porcupine since they liked the glue between plywood layers. The exterior siding was stained plywood. It looked better than it sounds. There were batten strips placed strategically, or randomly when they didn't have to conceal a seam. Nice effect--at least we thought so.

Each night as we slept those crazy glue-sniffing porcupines found the glue they loved.

One night Warren said, "I've had it." He grabbed his .22 and marched out the door in his underwear. (No, the door wasn't in Warren's underwear. Warren was, and thank you, Groucho Marx.) He turned on all the outdoor lights and marched clump clump clump outside. Shortly after that I heard, Ping! Ping!

"Oh, Lord. He's shot two of them." Ping. THREE. So many? Ping again, and then silence. Warren marched back into the house, still in his underwear, and stomped to the back door. He looked so determined that it was a sight you wouldn't want to laugh at.

"You killed four porcupines?"

"No, I missed." Out the back door again. PING! That was a serious Ping. In he came, smiling this time.

"I got the little bugger. I'll bury it tomorrow."

But not soon enough. When morning came, our dog Alice whined to go out, and without thinking we opened the door. Within a short time, we heard a yip. Dogs like dead varmints. A quill had entered Alice's nose. Poor dog. We had to take her to the vet for minor surgery.

The next time a porcupine entered our lives was a couple of years later.

PORCUPINE *II*

It was early spring. Warren had gone to Florida to help a friend build a house and make a few bucks. I was alone in the BARN (one of our Route 30 houses, and yes, I'll tell you about it soon) where we were living that particular winter. I didn't want to be all by myself back in the woods at that time of year.

It was night. Middle of. Probably 3:12 a.m. or so. I was sleeping.

Ah, there it was. That old familiar intermittent scratching. Different house. Same old plywood. Same old glue. Same old nice effect.

Now I knew what it was and went back to sleep. The following morning I inspected the scratching site. Sure enough. Same old toothmarks. What to do? No .22 for me. A "Have-A-Heart" trap? (It's the humane way to catch critters without killing them.) All you have to do is dispose of the caught animal. Somehow I couldn't envision my taking a drive with a trapped porcupine and coaxing him to leave me and go into the woods.

I pondered. If I smeared something on that spot which Old Porcupine found distasteful, so to speak, that could work. But what to smear? To the medicine chest. It took me only a few minutes to find my own "Have-A-

Heart": A brand new tube of Bengay. I taste-tested it and found it to be terrible indeed. I spread it thickly on the tooth-marked spots and beyond with a flat piece of wood.

That same night. Sleeping again. What's that I hear? Scratch scratch scratch. Silence. Scratch scratch after a few minutes. Silence. Scratch. Followed by a very long silence.

I was picturing a confused lone porcupine loping away up the hill.

Was Ben gay? Only his lover knew for sure.

In addition to glue, porcupines also like the taste of rubber. One of them ate the radiator hose in my car, putting it out of commission. I wondered how he reached it with all those quills in the way.

AND THEN THERE WERE MICE

It's really too cold for mice in Vermont for most of the year. They must prefer Maryland but many still lived in the north. As a result, when the outside temperature dipped below a certain degree, they knew how to find warmth. It doesn't seem to matter to a mouse where they find it.

One sunny fall day, Warren and I were driving along a quiet country road. Suddenly something caught our attention. On the outside of the windshield we saw a field mouse running from one side to the other close to the glass, pausing now and then to step over the wipers when they were in the way.

I feel it's important to interrupt this message to tell you what happened to these two Long Islanders after living in Vermont for just a short time. When we were flatlanders we treated all God's creatures with respect, if not downright love. But now we were seeing so MANY of God's four-legged creatures. Speaking of familiarity again, it didn't actually breed contempt. Maybe impatience. We just got, well, used to them, and thought a few less might improve our lives a bit. We were beginning to feel outnumbered.

As we drove along that fine sunny fall day, fascinated by the mouse as it sped by with the necessary pauses, Warren had a terrible idea. He turned on the wipers.

"It's a bird! It's a plane! It's SUPERMOUSE!"

MICE ARE NOT NICE

As a real estate broker, I was given the opportunity by my lake neighbors to rent their houses to prospective vacationers now and then.

One Saturday night a tenant who had come up from New Jersey that day called me. The husband had been lying on the couch and he told me he'd counted 27 mice as they ran by him.

I asked him, "All at once?"

"No, no," he replied. "One at a time."

Now common sense told me that unless there is an actual Fourth of July parade of mice marching through a living room, it just might very well be one mouse doing all that marching. I told him I'd be over in the morning to check it out.

When I got there the next day, the folks were packing to leave. His wife was mouse-phobic. I felt guilty and placed a trap in the kitchen after they left.

I caught one mouse. The other 26 may have stowed away in a suitcase and gone home with the folks.

I figured maybe the mice wanted to find out once and for all if it's true what they say about New Jersey.

Later that summer I had a thrill. I met Mickey Mouse.

Sitting in the kitchen of the kennel owners' home by myself one day I looked up and saw several mice running along the chair rail. One stopped dead in his tracks, turned and looked me in the eye. (His were crossed, incidentally.)

"Mickey! Why, you're Mickey Mouse, big black ears and all!" I'd never seen a mouse like him.

All the way to Vermont from Hollywood. And back.

I NEVER MET A SNAKE I LIKED

I may have this backwards, but a long time ago I understand there was a rattlesnake problem in Vermont. Black snakes were imported from somewhere to conquer and banish them. Or it may have been the other way around. First the black snakes and then the rattlers. Why the Vermonters would want either is beyond me.

Which brings me to my seeing something one day that most people have trouble believing when I tell them. Driving on the west side of Lake Bomoseen, near a slate quarry, I chanced upon a snake at least six inches in diameter and at least 12 feet long. Is that possible? Am I exaggerating? I stopped the car and didn't know if it was the conqueror or the conqueree. I just know that I was glad I was in a car. The snake was slithering across the road, and I couldn't see its snake eyes or its snake hips so I couldn't decide which was its back or its front. (Did it matter?) I only knew that I didn't want to drive *over* it and get all that gook on the underside of my car. I waited then until it had left me enough room to drive around one

89

end (which end? Must have been the back, right?) and I'm living to tell the story, which no one believes anyway because if I had actually seen it, wouldn't I have driven over the damn thing? Well, *I* wouldn't have and *I* didn't. Would you?

DITTO. NEITHER DID WARREN EVER MEET A SNAKE, ETC.

Asparagus grows in late spring, and when we were working on the house in Whiting, Warren discovered an asparagus patch across the road from the house. Ah! Such asparagus we ate four nights in a row! On the fifth day, Warren walked over with his penknife to cut some stalks for our dinner and came back empty-handed. His face was arranged in a grotesque mask in a pale shade of white.

"No more asparagus left?" I asked, as if I didn't know what he had found.

"I didn't see any."

"Really? All gone?"

"Mmmmmmmm. I met a snake."

Aside from that, the asparagus we had formerly eaten was the best we'd ever tasted.

HOW MUCH WOOD CAN A WOODCHUCK CHUCK?

We had a wonderful vegetable garden in Whiting. Remember those four beautiful acres? We planted a lot less than one of them to grow vegetables one summer. We had corn and tomatoes and melons and peppers and peas and stringbeans——but no potatoes.

Woodchucks love fresh homegrown vegetables. We did not love woodchucks for that reason. When we drove up from the lake to work in Whiting each morning, we began to find things missing, like lettuce and peppers. Upon inspection, Warren found two holes in the ground near the house. Aha! Could the woodchucks be living down there enjoying our vegetables? Betcha!

"I'm going to stick the garden hose down one hole and plug up the other and turn the water on and see what happens."

It shouldn't take too long to figure out what happened.

And it did. Talk about a drowned rat. Or, rather, a drowned woodchuck. He was both surprised and very wet.

What Warren did after that I'll never tell, but the rest of our vegetables grew until we were ready to harvest them. Oh, that Warren. The country boy.

HAPPY NEW YEAR!

THINGS GOT PRETTY FESTIVE on Lake Beebe during the Christmas holidays. Mary and Don Sondergeld always had a party on New Years Eve. All the vacation homeowners made sure they came to the lake around Christmas so they could catch some good skiing at Pico and Killington for a week or so.

What I remember about the Sondergelds' gala is the smell of wet wool, the clump of ski boots, the small puddles of melted snow on their kitchen floor, the wine that flowed like wine, the pretzels and potato chips, the almost-empty bowls of dip (why did we always get there late? Why? Why?), the ruddy faces of the young, the unfamiliar faces of the young, the familiar faces of the young which had become a year older in a year, the old familiar faces of the old, and music and laughter and good, good warm and friendly drinking fun all around.

Harry Chapin, the singer, owned a vacation home on the other side of the lake. One year, probably the winter before he was killed in an automobile accident on the Long Island Expressway, he and his wife Sandy brought a gang of kids, both theirs and friends of their kids, to Lake Beebe for the holidays.

All the lake people had been asked to "stop in." Our good friends Maris and Chick Ogg lived in Brandon in the winter and had come by for us to go to the parties. We four headed down to the lake to walk across on the two-foot-at-least thick ice to join the Chapin gang.

Now Chick Ogg was Mr. Dapper, and I can still see him walking gingerly——now stepping, now sliding——in his L. L. Bean Wellington boots and his Tan L. L. Bean Classic Fit Eight-wale Country Corduroy Trousers with the Pleated Front and the 1-1/2 Inch Belt Loops and Requiring Minimal Ironing. Without Cuffs. I don't think his camel hair finger-tip-length coat came from L. L. Bean. It probably came from New Jersey, from whence he and Maris had come.

When we got to the Chapins' the living room was filled with kids, and the host was acting out a charades word or phrase and the kids were stumped. We mingled and sipped some wine and left for the Sondergelds and the sour cream dip that was probably *all* gone by now.

I wonder if L. L. Bean still makes those Wellington boots.

WE SPENT A LONG WEEKEND THERE ONE NIGHT

WARREN DIDN'T HAVE THE SAME YEARNING for the ocean that I did, but he was willing to drive over to Maine whenever I needed a saltwater fix.

We knew little about the coast of Maine, having spent some vacation time in the Belgrade Lakes Region of the state and not having taken a ride east to the ocean to see if it looked like the one we'd left off the south shore of Long Island.

One Saturday we drove from Vermont to Maine, and New Hampshire was in between. It took us three hours to get to the bottom town on the coast of Maine where we wanted to wander northward until we hit a town we fell in love with. We saw several signs advertising The Cliff House and it sounded expensive because it was right on the ocean, but by the time we drove back and forth a few times and found our cranky selves snapping at each other in impatience, we said, "What the heck, as long as we're here for the ocean, let's spring for The Cliff House!" Budget be damned. And in we drove through a grove of pine trees until we came upon a beautiful white rambling building with weathered shutters.

We registered for a room overlooking the ocean, unpacked our tacky duffel bags at which our lovely room laughed, poured two glasses of wine and headed for the rocks at the shore below us. What a sight! And as the waves pounded the rocks and sent the spray up to where we sat, we concluded we had died and gone to heaven. We watched the boats chugging out there, some of which were pulling in lobster traps, which told us, "It's lobster tonight or nothin'!"

The clerk at the desk recommended another big expense, the finest restaurant in town, and there was dancing later in the lounge as well. We ate, and we danced until the wee small hours. The next morning we walked the Marginal Way in Ogunquit after an expensive breakfast, ate lunch at a fine, not-too-expensive restaurant overlooking the ocean, and even got into the ocean at Ogunquit beach at 3 p.m. when the sun was the strongest but the water was probably no warmer than 61 degrees, alas! But the salt revived my soul!

We had charged a ton of money to our credit card but on the way home we agreed that it was a wonderful change of pace from our Vermont working life, that we deserved every moment of it, and in reality, after having packed in so many tourist events in a short span of time, that we had indeed spent a long weekend there one night. We also sprang for and packed in a few lobsters to take home to be boiled for our eating pleasure the next night.

While I was writing about this, I referred to my AAA tour book for Maine and couldn't find The Cliff House listed. I may have imagined the name or it just wasn't listed with AAA, or it may just have gone the way of all beautiful privately-owned hotels overlooking the ocean in that part of the world.

BOOTS AND HAT

I LOVE CLOTHES. When I saw those deep cherry leather cowboy boots at Dexters in Rutland, did I dare buy them? A woman my age? In her fifties?

I bought them. I loved them. That night I put them in front of the television set so I could look at them while I watched a rerun of *Mash* and more.

When I finally got up the courage to wear them to the real estate office——The Riley Agency in Castleton——I kept my feet under my desk as long as I could. The door opened late one morning and in walked a young man and a young woman. He was wearing a great big cowboy hat, which he tipped when he walked into the room. The two of them sat down to talk to Sally Sheldon, one of the insurance agents, and because everyone was busy I took that opportunity to walk past them to pull something from a file drawer. But the man looked up as I passed him. Then he looked down. At my feet.

"I like yer boots."

"Thanks. I like yer hat."

He continued to talk to Sally. I walked back to my desk.

Two cowboys meet in Vermont. The smell of sagebrush hung in the air.

DANCING IN THE DARK

OUR SOCIAL LIFE IN THE WINTER and summer was pretty lively. Vacation people flooded the area and we were never without dates. Their place or ours.

But in the spring and the fall, the flooding became a trickle. We locals had to gather together to remember how to interact with other human beings, and one of my favorite gatherings was the annual Lakes Region dinner-dance for the local business people.

Each year the event was held at a nearby resort or restaurant. One I recall with fondness was held at the Inn at Lake St. Catherine where we had dinner, but no dancing. However, there was an old-fashioned upright player piano in the lounge with some more or less up to date rolls of music if anybody felt like pumping and singing. I wanted to try to sound like Carly Simon on *Nobody Does It Better.* A 12-year-old girl and I sang our hearts out. She was good but I was better, but neither of us sounded like Carly Simon.

The best of those dinner-dances was held at the Trak-in-Seen Inn at Lake Bomoseen one year. We'd been invited to have cocktails and to watch the Kentucky Derby at Tom and Barbara Degnen's home before we all went to dinner. Then dinner. Then dancing. And one of the women at our table remarked, "Warren, you should take Elaine out more. She looks as if she's saved up all that dancing for years!"

And dance I did. With anyone and everyone, including Warren. The music was canned and the floor was smooth and big enough and the lights were low, and I danced and danced and danced for about two hours straight.

When Warren was finally able to drag me home, it was about midnight, and he took his ice cream to bed and left me with the radio, which I turned on at once. At that time of the morning, all kinds of great music can be coaxed from the radio from stations all around the country, so I took off my shoes, turned out the lights, and with just the glow of the big old stereo/radio throwing my shadow on the walls and ceiling, I danced in the dark.

Around and around on the carpeted floor I danced. Was I wired? Had I indeed had all that dancing saved up for all those years? You bet! And every time a slow number came on, Warren would rouse himself out of the bed and come in to the living room and dance with me. It was very romantic and sweet. By around three o'clock, my wheels fell off and I took off the rest of my clothes, got into my jammies, didn't wash my face or brush my teeth, and crawled into bed with Warren. We probably slept until at least nine.

I couldn't understand why I wasn't tired that morning, and I couldn't wait for the next Lakes Region Vermont dinner-dance.

LOCAL POLITICS IN VERMONT

WE WERE ABLE TO CATCH three channels on television during our Vermont life. When we were living at the Hubbardton Gulf house we delighted in CBS, NBC and ABC. But we delighted even more at Lake Beebe because we traded ETV (Educational Television—or as it's known on Long Island, Channel 13) for ABC and felt very lucky. Warren had climbed a tall aspen and had attached an antenna way up there, turned it now right, now left, while I yelled from the living room, "That's good, Oh, that's better. No, not so good. Yes! Stay right there!" (Sounds a little obscene.) Then I moved the dial to the point where another fuzzy picture appeared on the screen. We then repeated the turning and the yelling two more times.

I know. You'd been wondering what we did all day up there in the woods.

Once we were blessed with public television, I sat down in my favorite chair in the living room and watched Masterpiece Theater every Sunday night at nine o'clock. And that's when I discovered my passion for politics. The presentation was *Disraeli,* starring Ian McShane, who was a hunk in those days. I don't know if it was the hunk or the program that sparked my interest, and London was a far cry from Hubbardton, but Hubbardton was closer and I was hooked. What is that saying? "Think globally. Act locally."

In the spring of 1979, we were visited by the three listers of the town of Hubbardton. A lister is a tax assessor, and the three men came to see if we had made any physical improvements to our home during the year, the better to tax us for, my dear.

As they were leaving I asked the man named Victor Brewer how a person became a lister because this was something I felt I might like to do. Victor said he'd be in touch with me because the term of one of the men was almost over and he wasn't planning to run again. It was an elected position, and in November Victor asked me to sign a consent that my name be placed on the ballot on Town Meeting Day in March. He circulated a petition then, and after getting the required number of signatures my name was placed on the ballot for a three-year term. I knew I was a shoo-in. Who would want such a job besides me, who was developing a taste for politics?

I was elected, and my stint as town lister became one of the best experiences I had during my Vermont life.

TOWN OF HUBBARDTON LISTER

Victor and I met on April first in the old schoolhouse on Route 30 in Hubbardton, and he explained what our task would be for the next month or so. We received $3 an hour and kept a record of our time. After being sworn in by the Town Clerk, and after Victor told me that the third lister, John Carey, was ill and may not be able to join us for a "day or two," Vic, as most everyone called him, familiarized me with the present record keeping system: a file box containing a 5 x 7 card for each property in Hubbardton. It wasn't too long before I began to feel a creeping sense of perplexity because I could see the numbers on the cards seemed to have no relation to any other number on the rest of the cards in the box.

"Why," I asked, "is this property listed as $3,000 when most properties in the town are now selling in the $25,000 to $60,000 range?" He told me because that $3,000 had been that way for many years and there was no reason to change it. (Say what?) As I explored further, I saw most properties were listed at anywhere from $1000 to $15,000, and those in the higher range were invariably those owned by vacation people who lived out of state because "they're newer." (What, again?)

Vic was an adorable 80-year-old man, formerly having lived on Long Island, and I don't know to this day whether he was an adorable, retired, elegant gentleman who had an air of innocence about him, or whether he was adorable and elegant and dumb like a fox.

The numbers on the cards remained the same for the first year of my job, and if a property had transferred we'd go take a look at the outside of the house and eyeball the land measurements, and since it was "newer," the number would be raised on the card so that it would be in line with the other new properties, mostly vacation homes. As I'm writing this, my head is spinning, because without any experience I had little say in the matter, and what kind of job was I actually doing? I knew something was wrong but hadn't figured out a way to start straightening it out. Good thing I was making only $3 an hour! That's all I was worth that first year.

After we'd finished with the 5 x 7 cards, we mailed out Change of Appraisal notices to the new owners. We advised them of the date for Grievance Day that year. The schedule of recourse is set by the state according to the size of the town. We posted the necessary notices in the required five sites in town. At that time, there were about 450 residents and 750 properties in Hubbardton, and the town is 36 square miles, or six by six miles. Grievance Day was set for the first Tuesday in May and perhaps three people came to air their grievances. After we'd consulted with John Carey we made our decisions and sent out the Result of Grievance Day Appeal to the three families. One party took their appeal to the Board of Civil Authority (made up of five town selectmen and four justices of the peace, all elected offices) who then voted to lower the appraisal. If the taxpayer was still not satisfied with the appraisal number, the next step was either to appeal to the Vermont Department of Taxation and Finance or appeal to the courts. If they appealed to the Tax board, three appraisers would come to town by appointment, and the listers and the Board of Civil Authority would be present, along with the taxpayer, and we'd all try to persuade the appraisers! It then took six months to hear the results. It was common knowledge that to appeal to the courts was more advantageous because the judge usually voted in favor of the taxpayer. But for reasons best known to the taxpayer, most people opted for the former, and maybe because it cost the taxpayer $10 instead of $20, but it also took longer.

Vic and I then sat down together with our records and listed all the properties in the Grand List, a really grand, important-looking leather-bound loose-leaf binder, affixed our signatures and placed the book in the Town Clerk's office and it became a part of the public record. The Grand List was now available for viewing by all the taxpayers if they so wished. When summer arrived, the selectmen met and designed a budget, including those items which had been voted on at Town Meeting in March, divided the budget by the Grand List and came up with the tax rate. The tax bills were sent out by August to the taxpayers. By multiplying the tax rate by 1% of the appraisal on each property, the amount of tax was arrived at, and there was no penalty if the tax was paid by October 1.

I have to say here that I think this whole system is a work of art. This is probably going on in many towns throughout the country but I'm aware of its existence only in Vermont and I was happy to be such a large part of it in one small town. It's what I like to think of as democracy in action.

The listers' work was finished for the year, but with all that time on my hands I got Vic's permission to try to streamline those 5 x 7 cards from which we'd be working the following spring. The present cards had the taxpayers names, a description of the property (for instance, "the Hubbard place," which had served the listers well for many years, I was sure, but there was no notation of the location in all those 36 square miles) and the appraisal amount. With the help of a map and one of our cars, Vic and I determined the location of all, or almost all, the properties, and by combining the transfers which had taken place on a property since 1970, when the Vermont transfer tax went into law, we now had an abstract on the property along with other pertinent information necessary to do next year's work. During the ensuing months as I was getting things in order, I kept thinking that if Victor Brewer died suddenly, he'd be taking more data to his grave than had been on those cards.

Little did I know I was opening a Pandora's Box.

Victor the Innocent

YEAR TWO, TOO

ON TOWN MEETING DAY THE following March, the town voted to buy a brand new fire engine (green, not red) and to pay for it in one year. When April first arrived, the listers assembled in the school house, and Victor and I were joined by a new member, Bob Bowen, who had been elected in March to take the place of John Carey, who had died the previous fall.

This was my second year, and with the information I'd gathered by redesigning the record keeping system, I slowly began to see some inequities present in the appraisals. Bob was also questioning the lack of a frame of reference, having been a real estate broker in New York State for several years. Vic saw us ganging up on him, but he was unflappable and merely batted his eyelids more often and even more becomingly. Slowly we tried some minor adjusting but we began to see that major surgery would be required eventually. Not knowing where to start--this would become an almost daunting task--we stayed our current course and submitted the Grand List on time. We held Grievance Day with very little activity and Vic, Bob and I gradually went back to our separate and mostly peaceful lives.

But we didn't know what was in store for us when the tax rate was determined. Can you imagine what a $50,000 green (or even red) fire engine in a rather simple budget can do to a tax rate?

The tax bills were sent out in August as usual, and the local folks saw only a slight rise in their taxes because of their low appraisals. The vacation property owners in the past had not been unhappy to pay their usually low taxes to their adopted state of Vermont--they were ridiculously low compared to their home state's--but the sleeping dogs woke up with a start and were barking like mad. As it turned out, fewer than half the taxpayers in the town were paying over 80% of the taxes. And we all know who was to blame. Those darn listers, of course.

But that was only the beginning.

TARRED AND FEATHERED

APRIL 1, 1982, SAW THREE LISTERS who knew it was time to come out fighting--two of us were ready, anyway. Vic was still smiling and batting those eyelids. This was to be my third year. It was Bob's second, and Victor had just been elected to another three years. Bob and I knew we had to do our best in ridding the list of inequities. The three of us argued and agonized, and Bob and I agreed, and Victor was reluctant, to put all the properties on an equal footing. We would have to reappraise the whole town in order to do this. Were we qualified? Well, Bob and I had real estate experience, and Vic said he'd go along for the ride. And what a ride it was!

First, we took a long hard look at the transfer records and found that the average ratio of appraisal to Fair Market Value (FMV) ranged between 12% and 18% on those properties recently bought or sold, with some "older" properties as low as 4% of FMV and "newer" ones as high as 50% of FMV. More discussions followed and finally, after a few yelling bouts which were just short of punches in the nose, we came up with placing a fair market figure on every property in the town by comparing recent sales figures and placing a comparable number on the older properties. We would then take 15% of the FMV across the board. Why did we pick 15%? This was our method of easing up to 100% of FMV which the state had just decreed every town must appraise at by a deadline two years hence in order to qualify for state aid to education.

Then we hit the road to see each and every property in town. (When we were able to see the humor in our serious task, Bob nicknamed us The Eyeball Appraisal Company, because as we set out for the day, we designated some of the properties as those we would just "eyeball." To inspect the interiors of at least 250 houses this time around would have been too exhausting a task.)

As we drove from property to property, each of us jotted down a "guesstimate" of the property's value according to what we could see, along with the acreage involved. With our experience, Bob's and my jotted numbers came within a couple of thousand dollars of the other, and Vic's were either ten to twenty thousand dollars off from ours in either direction. Then another argument would happen over and over again, and we would try to come up with a compromise, but not too! We'd return to our table at the schoolhouse, armed with our numbers and my calculator, and punch in 15% of the number to come up with the appraisal figure. (We were definitely earning our $3 an hour by now.)

When all the driving around was completed, and the calculating process was finished, we murmured a small prayer and sent out Change of Appraisal notices to almost every property owner in Hubbardton. We also included what we considered to be a well-thought-out letter with each notice to explain what we'd done and why. We knew the taxpayers were all good sports and would understand and we'd all live happily ever after.

Our phones never stopped ringing. We received proposed duel dates besides the 63 grievance letters, which were fewer than 10% of the taxpayers, which surprised us. We lowered many of the appraisals after considering their appeals. About 35 of those went on to the Board of Civil Authority, and they lowered some and even raised a few!

Throughout this whole period we had tried to keep close contact with the Selectmen to keep them informed of our intentions because we knew that without their support we could be tarred and feathered and run out of town. And they were more inclined to be open to this big change once we enlisted their aid.

Despite our aim to create a more just Grand List, I know that we made very few friends that year. Even those whose appraisals had been lowered were angry. They thought their status should be retroactive! (We'd been told by our representative from the Taxation Board that the reappraisal of a town usually resulted in 1/3 of the appraisals going higher than before, 1/3 would go lower and 1/3 would remain the same).

By summer of that year, the grand leather-bound Grand List binder in the Town Clerk's Office was dog-eared, frayed and ragged from the conscientious scrutiny of those taxpayers who had to find out what their neighbors had been taxed.

During the course of my term as lister in Vermont I'd been told by many taxpayers that they didn't mind paying taxes so long as the system was equitable. But now that it was as equitable and as fair as we could make it, I'm not so sure that that's true for some taxpayers. Perhaps people just downright resent paying taxes because there's no such thing as fair when it comes to money.

I also realized that most taxpayers know very little about the tax process, and tax rates and tax bases in general, as was I back on Long Island. It seems most of the citizenry in any county, hamlet or city wouldn't want such a thankless job--not if popularity counts--and finding fault just naturally comes with the territory.

I was exposed to a lot of human nature during those three years, and especially in that last year. I saw quiet folks become tigers. I encountered tigers who became reasonable, and a few of the citizens who I thought had integrity had a streak of con-artist in them.

Surprise! I decided not to run again. Victor had a mild stroke during May, hung in as long as he could, and retired from the position at the end of August. Bob knew he couldn't face another year without his buddies and submitted his resignation before Christmas. That meant, of course, that the Selectmen had to appoint two new listers, but that's another story, and one that I won't tell!

Many of us thought that things would revert to the good old days, but too much had changed for the system to go back to the way it was before. I moved out of Vermont in 1984, and I've heard that with the guidance of the Department of Taxation and Finance the later listers were making use of the standard appraisal cards (size 8-1/2 x 11) and are trying to inspect more properties both inside and out every year.

I still look back on those listing days as being happy days. Those guys—Vic and Bob--were great to work with, and I think we were a good team. Even though the job was taxing, so to speak, somehow we were able to see the humor as it cropped up, and crop up it did! I loved being a big fish in a small pond, and I discovered an integrity in myself that I didn't know I had.

Politics can be an art form. There's danger, though, if citizens place too much trust in their elected officials. (May I refer you to our present administrations in Washington and Albany?)

We seem to be too willing to let someone else take care of running the place. But when an official is not kept accountable, I learned first hand how tempting it is to abuse the power with which we've been entrusted. (Oh, don't get me started!)

In the little town of Hubbardton, then, I learned about politics in Vermont. To experience it on such a small and manageable scale, I began to understand and appreciate it both nationally and globally.

Incidentally, I saw Ian McShane a while back in a *West Wing* rerun. Yeah, he's still hunk material, but I'd forgotten about his voice's lovely nasal quality!

ARLINE

HOW DID SO MANY INTERESTING PEOPLE find our corner of Vermont? We certainly met a bunch. Even a few famous ones whose names you may recognize.

Howell and Susan Raines was a lovely young couple from Virginia. They were gentle, genteel and Southern and they were renting a home on the lake for a few weeks one summer. They had asked me about restaurants in the area. Of course, I had to tell them about the Dog Team, just north of Middlebury.

In earlier years, the building which was now the restaurant had been a trading post. Hence, the Dog Team. John Joy was the owner and his mother and father had started the business some years before. Hungry folk from miles around still frequented the spot, and there was usually a wait for a table, especially on weekends. The food was simple and delicious and served family style.

The menu rarely changed and there were perhaps five or six entrees from which to choose. (When we first started going there the fried chicken dinner was $2.95. It has since gone up.) Then there were the sticky buns, and I suspect they were the big draw. That was what people mentioned when the Dog Team was. Mrs. Lounsbury was the hostess who greeted the customers as they entered the lounge. Next to her was the chalk board on which were written the entrees, but Mrs. Lounsbury asked each patron as the line moved forward their choice of appetizer: New England clam chowder or apple ci-der, and I can still hear her saying "sy-der" with the pause between syllables.

Arline was our favorite waitress. She was a tall woman, sturdily built, and we always hoped she would be our waitress because she had a dry sense of humor and made us laugh when she said something under her breath which was meant for our ears only. Arline played on the restaurant's softball team when she wasn't working, and as friendly and helpful as she was, I saw her as a no-nonsense woman.

"We went to the Dog Team last night." I met Howell and Susan walking on the lake road the next morning.

"How was dinner?" I asked.

Arline had waited on them and reality had met their expectations. The food was tasty and the service exceptional. When Arline asked if they needed anything more, the gentle, genteel Susan drawled, "My husband would like more mashed potatoes."

Now. Arline probably thought a grown man should be able to ask for his own mashed potatoes, forgetting for a moment that North and South have different customs still.

But Arline smiled her broad inimitable smile, and without skipping a beat, she pulled herself up to her almost six feet and replied, "Oh, he *would,* would he?"

Arline brought Howell his mashed potatoes.

* * * *

During the summer following Warren's death, this same special couple invited me for dinner across the lake at what was then Harry and Sandy Chapin's vacation home. The Raineses were staying there, and that night Howell's folks and their cousins joined us around the table. Not only was I bathed in Southern Comfort—all those gentle Southerners drawling softly and warming me—but the Raines's 10-year-old son charmed us all with his break-dancing while his older brother supplied the music via cassette tape.

I'm sure we had mashed potatoes that night, too.

OUR FATHER, WHO

A ONE-DAY REAL ESTATE seminar was held at one of the Killington ski resorts in March one year. The usual amount of snow covered the ground the farther up the mountain I drove, but the snow had stopped falling mid-morning and all I had to worry about was that it might start again before I had to drive home that evening.

It didn't though, and I called Warren to let him know I was on my way after our early dinner closing the seminar. It was a 45-minute drive to Hubbardton.

The snow was disappearing as I got closer to Rutland. When I continued on Route 4 to start the now ten-mile drive to Castleton Corners, all that remained after that was the ten miles north on Route 30. Piece o' cake. But there are no lights on that stretch of Route 4 as it climbs steadily and then levels off.

I think it's only fair to tell you that Vermont has a lot of weather. I've already talked about the snow, but when I finally let it sink in that we were in a snow belt and that where there's snow there's gotta be rain, which I've already mentioned with the tap tap tapping on the car roof in spring. Yes, we had a lot of snow and we had a lot of rain. Those bright sunny clear wonderful days that bring a smile to my heart today were so rare that we all got together to talk about them. Of course, they were the brightest, the sunniest, the clearest and the most wonderful days I'd seen anywhere, so they were talk-worthy indeed.

Fog was also on the weather menu. Fog came in on slippered feet and there I was on Route 4 suddenly and totally surrounded by that old debbil fog with its slippers still on. March is famous/notorious for fog. It's caused by the snow and the warmer air and something called inversion and I'm no meteorologist as I've already confessed and I don't care what anybody says.

It was too late to turn back because I was on a two-lane highway way up high, and the two lanes were going west, and the two lanes on the other side of the divide were heading east and those were about ten feet lower than the two lanes heading west on which I was driving at that particular time. Fog to the left of me. Fog to the right of me. Fog over my head and beneath me. The only reason I could see the hand in front of my face was because my hand was in the fog-free car with me.

I slowed down to a slow, crawling, creeping motion. Did I have fog lights? No. Should I put the high beams on? No, I'd been told that was worse. Regular ol' beams? Parking lights? I settled for regular. My only comforting thought was that no car could hit me head on or vice versa.

I'd just discovered that singing soothed me when I got scared. Did I sing a sprightly tune in my current fog dilemma? My music selection for that night was the *Lord's Prayer,* and the line I met and stayed with over and over (and over) was, *Give us this day our daily bread*—and I said, not yesterday's or tomorrow's, but today's. When I hear that little girl voice 20 years later, I hear wussy, but it was all I could manage in the singing department that scary night.

By the time I got to my turnoff ten miles later, I left the fog on the mountain and made it home safe and almost sound, wondering the while how long it would take for those fingernail marks on my palms to go away.

Warren was worrying, of course, and what was taking me the almost two hours to get home because Lake Beebe was fogless, but I bet him he hadn't been as worried as I up there on the mountain, poking along at three miles an hour, tops, and keeping an eye on that line on my left and watching my hand in front of my face so that I could put it into my mouth, nails first. And singing a little religious number.

Oh, if cellular phones had been around back then he could have kept me company as I worried myself home.

I GET AROUND

I WAS NAÏVE ENOUGH IN THOSE DAYS to think all Vermonters would succumb to my charms and a few might even eventually clasp me to their bosoms. I can tell you about two who didn't.

Mud season arrives in Vermont somewhere between winter and summer. It's usually a welcome relief because the threat of snow has passed and can spring be far behind? The ground begins to thaw during the day, and then freezes again at night as the temperature drops. This takes place over the course of several weeks. (And then of course on the heels of mud season comes bug season, just when you thought it was safe to go out again because the weather has turned almost balmy. So be it.)

A standard mud season arrived as anticipated one spring, and I ventured forth to visit a local farmer one day. I probably had to see him about a property with regard to my listing chores, because I didn't ordinarily visit a local farmer unless he had potatoes he wanted to sell. I had no trouble finding his house out there in the fields, and I met no mud along the way. I could see it was clear sailing to his house.

I spoke to him while he stood framed by his front door, and then I made the mistake of asking him, "If I drive out that way (different from where I'd come in) is it pretty clear?"

"Oh, yes," he assured me. "Just drive around that bend and you'll be fine." Go ahead, you stupid city slicker babe. Do it.

Just around that bend, of course, was the biggest mud mess I'd seen so far.

"Damn you, Billy Gordon," I heard myself saying because I couldn't turn around and go back the other way. There was room for only one car and I had to go forward.

"Okay, wise guy, if I get stuck you can come pull me out of this mud after you've had your big laugh."

I backed up quickly, and then took a flying leap into the wild unknown, gunning that little engine for all it was worth, and by damn, I barreled through, spewing mud all over the place as the car rocked from side to side but never stopped.

"Yea! I'm getting good!" I yelled out loud. "Another year in this place and I'll qualify for something, even if it's only Flatlander Who Can Get Through Mud!" I knew I'd never qualify for Vermonter-hood because one has to be born into that elite distinction.

It gave me some satisfaction, though, to know that the smile was slowly leaving Billy's face as he watched me chugging on down the road.

THE DAMN DAM

THE NEXT TIME I was made a fool of was during the January thaw the following year. Oh, there was lots of snow, but it was getting old and no new stuff had come down for a week. It was bright overhead and I was prepared to drive up to Lake Hortonia to check on the location of a vacation property that had come on the market a few weeks earlier.

I found the property on my map. It was just a number in a vague setting, so I had to stop to ask directions at the general store on the west shore of the frozen lake.

Ginny Hawthorne owned the store, and I thought I looked friendly when I asked her where the Baxter place was.

"Oh," she said, "I don't know exactly where it is but I think it's over there a ways back from the lake. But I can't tell you exactly where it is."

"How can I get there?"

"You'll have to get over to the other side of the lake by walking across the dam," and she paused to point casually in a southwesterly northeasterly direction, "and then walk through the woods until you come to it. But I think it's over there someplace." She pointed again waving her whole hand. Casual all the way she was.

I tried to keep that friendly smile on my face, as she tried to keep that friendly smile on her face at the same time. (Come to think of it, I think we were both talking through our teeth to/at each other.)

"Thank you so much, Ginny," I said as I went out the door.

"Okay, Elaine, where to now?" I asked myself under my breath.

It was easy walking across the dam. The ice had melted and I could get a firm footing with my stylish fur-topped boots with the sturdy tread. There was no danger because on either side was solid ice with at least a foot of snow on top of that.

117

I minced fearlessly on until I got to the woods, where it was a little tougher going. I had to lift each foot up to here to clear the depth of snow because there was a slick of ice on top--at least an inch on top of at least 12 inches of snow--and I crunched slowly along, now left foot up, now down, now right foot up, now down, looking for a camp with a real estate sign near it.

Now crunch right. Now crunch left without falling into the crust with the snow underneath. Balance was the key here and I tried to keep mine by holding my arms out straight from the sides of my body, like a tightrope walker? Up and down my feet went but I didn't fall. I found nothing. Back a ways from the lake, she said? I kept going and when I was about to give up and come back maybe in July, I spotted the sign. I trudged the several yards to the house and stopped to take a look around to get my bearings. The sun's rays were now coming through the tree branches overhead and I was standing smack dab on the edge of the frozen lake. I stood in front of it then and looked across the 100 yards to the other side to see the general store in all its treacherous glory.

Son of a gun. Ginny was probably looking at the camp when she was giving me those non-directions (and the business). Now I could picture her standing back from the window, peeking out so I couldn't see her, snickering to herself and muttering, Ha ha, you dumb New York broad.

I didn't bother to stop and say goodbye-and-thank-you before I got in the car and drove away.

By the way, all names have been changed to protect the wicked.

Elaine Polson Shiber

DINNER AT THE FAIR HAVEN INN

OUR FRIENDS MARIS AND CHICK OGG and we had plenty of time in the spring, fall and winter months to socialize with each other, and for some reason our times together usually involved food and plenty of it. They owned Uncle Charlie's Restaurant on the eastern shore of Lake Bomoseen, which was open from late spring until the fall, after which that part of Vermont went into hibernation. They lived downstairs at the restaurant during the summer, and worked when they weren't playing in or on the lake.

Maris was the super chef and Chick was the charming maitre d' and business manager. When they weren't restaurateurs, we ate dinner at their house and didn't have to pay, and when Warren and I entertained them we worked day and night for a week to put something on the table that wouldn't embarrass us.

Every once in a while, though, we went out for dinner, and one of the restaurants that served in the off-season was the Fair Haven Inn, which was in a stately old white former home on the square in Fair Haven, the town maybe 15 miles southwest of us. The owner was Johnny, and a few members of his family worked with him. They were Greeks and served many fine Greek dishes.

Off the four of us went one night to Fair Haven, walked into the restaurant and met not a soul and a lot of silence. Just as we thought it was time to leave, a young man came out from the back, stopped us and told us the restaurant was closed, but could we wait a minute? He wanted to talk to Johnny. When he came back he asked if we would like Johnny to prepare us a meal, that he would like to create something special and Greek for us. We all nodded yes!

The young man seated us and then brought out ouzo for our drinking pleasure and more ouzo for our further drinking pleasure and then he started to bring out the most wonderful Greek dishes, starting with a gorgeous Greek appetizer or two, and then a stunning Greek entrée or four because they came in different sizes and more ouzo just for the hell of it, and all the while each little dish was a surprise and that was a good thing because we never could have ordered such luscious food even if we knew how to pronounce it. I'm sure we had dessert, and yet I'm not sure, but if we did it was probably the one with the apples in it which ends in *–lava*, accent on the *–va*. We ran out of ouzo once in a while so the server knew he should bring out more for our later drinking pleasure which we never seemed to get to the bottom of.

And then! When we could still see straight and make out another figure walking toward us, who should appear but Johnny carrying a mandolin—-or was it a balalaika? He drew up a chair---or was it the floor?—-and sat down and grinned at us loopy people—-104 women and 273 men, all cockeyed—-and played his Greek music for us for at least three days—-or was it an hour or less?—-and we got the bill and said, Wow! What a bargain! and let's have one more ouzo for the road, and tipsied out to the train—-or was it a bus?—-and should have pushed the car all the way home because certainly none of us was in any condition to drive, but fortunately we were the only ones on the road for the 15 or so miles home and we arrived safely, I think, because here I am today writing about that night of nights on the town.

Whew!

And thank you, Johnny!

CHOONEY

THAT'S NOT HER REAL NAME. "Chooney" is the name I gave June Sherline some years after I left Vermont. It started out as "June," then it became "Choon," which naturally became "Chooney." I introduced you to her back there with the word "intrepid," when she described the Gallaghers. Now I think it's only fair to give you a larger picture of this special woman.

Let me tell you a few anecdotes first. (A little background music, please.)

One summer day I'd left the office in Castleton and suddenly Route 30 and everywhere else in the area was hit with one of the most severe thunderstorms I'd seen in Vermont. In fact lightning hit our television at home while Warren watched in fear as the bolt streaked across the floor. And, as they say, there was local flooding by overflowing local rivers and streams. I had trouble seeing the rain- and wind-swept road in front of me and finally had to pull over to wait for the storm to subside, as did most other travelers on Route 30 as I joined the line of cars doing the same thing by the side of the road. Not all the travelers, though. For speeding up the highway was a car I knew well. June and Ruth whizzed by me and I thought, "Intrepid. There she goes!"

One February Warren and I stopped on the coast of South Carolina to see June and Ruth on our way to Florida. They knew it was smart to go south and stay there for the winter. Before they served us a deliciously typical JuneandRuth coastal South Carolina meal, the four of us did a little before-dinner drinking and danced to a tape until we got hungry. It was the *Christmas Jollies* (Christmas had come and gone two months earlier but who cared?) by the *Salsoul Orchestra,* and you may know the tape. I call it *Sacred Christmas Carols to Dance Your Buns Off By.*

Speaking of dancing, one night the four of us went to the Somewhere Restaurant and Bar just outside Fair Haven where a band played country and western music, and we danced and danced for a few hours, maneuvering around the men wearing 10-gallon hats. There was a cute guy in white and black high top sneakers who didn't want to stop dancing—-ever-—and one by one he asked June or Ruth or me to dance with him.

When he finally got to me and we were dancing up a storm, he said, "You folks aren't from around here, are you?"

I answered, "Sure we are!"

"Oh, yeah? Where do you live?" Suspicious, he was.

"Hubbardton."

I don't know if he believed me or not, but it didn't seem to matter because he danced with one of us the rest of the night.

Now for the June story. (Drum roll, please.)

When June was in her twenties, she realized she needed some fresh air in the form of a new life. She was living in metropolitan New York and saw a newspaper ad for a couple of kids' camps for sale. Hmmmm, she thought, and then found herself on the subway tracking down the real estate firm behind the ad. She was also thinking, "Hmmmm. How can I think about buying *anything,* let alone a kids' camp? All I have to my name is a Persian lamb coat, a couple of bonds, and my old Plymouth."

There were two operating camps for sale in Vermont: Camp Awanee on Lake Beebe, a girls camp, and Twin Lakes Camp on Echo Lake, a boys camp, and since they were separated only by Route 30 and close to each other, they were the perfect solution for families who wanted to send their kids of both genders to camp at the same time in almost the same place.

The broker suggested to June that this might be just what she should buy. During the purchase transaction she could work alongside the present owners to create a smooth transition for all, including the parents, who as June has told me, are usually reluctant to change the existing happy camp arrangements for their kids. Now with June easing herself into eventually running the camp, their fears would be assuaged and they'd know their kids would be well taken care of by this neat new woman.

Back on the subway. The price seemed right and all she needed was $15,000 for a down payment. *Fifteen Thousand Dollars!* Even with the sale of the coat and the car, with the bonds thrown in, all she could probably scrape together would be $1,000, if that. And she'd have no car and no coat.

I don't have to tell you how June managed to borrow the $15,000--$5,000 from three sources——and to pay it back within a year because I know how smart she is, how resourceful she is, and how much she really wanted to fly on her own when she was a mere wisp of a lass of 26. Remember, too, that she's special. Trust me. She got the $15,000, and got a mortgage for the rest.

For 25 years June owned and ran those two camps and eventually had at Awanee alone horses, a stable, canoes, rowboats, oars, a chef and 40 counselors, plus a kitchen crew of eight, 14 waitresses and an infirmary with a doctor and a nurse on call at all times, and then there was the attendance which averaged about 150 girls each summer. The lake was surrounded by small neat brown buildings with bunks, and there was a boat not unlike the African Queen which was called the Beebe Queen, of course, on which tea was served on special afternoons all summer long as it floated by.

June never took a vacation during those years because for 16 of them she owned a girls school in New York City and ran that in the winter. She taught there, too, in her spare time.

They don't make people like her any more.

After 25 years June decided she was ready to live another kind of life and had the Lake Beebe acreage subdivided and one by one all the parcels were sold, one of which became ours.

When Warren and I met June in 1964, she was living in the house at the head of the lake from which she'd managed the girls camp. She eventually sold it and had a marvelous sprawling ranch house built on the other end of the lake, where her friend Ruth, whom she'd known since their teens and with whom she became reacquainted some years later, joined her. The two of them became the Hostesses with the Mostesses on Lake Beebe, no matter what anyone tells you. Lobster and Manhattans and turkey and ham and Martinis and stuffing, shrimp and Old Fashioneds, clams on the half shell and Clams Casino, roast beef and potato chips, wine and dips galore and plenty of laughs. June is one of the funniest story tellers I know, no matter what *she* tells you, and if my memory hadn't forsaken me I'd tell you a story or two of hers right now.

When I came home from California after spending almost two months with my kids to heal after Warren's death, June and Ruth arranged to pick me up at the Amtrak station in Whitehall, N.Y., and then drive me home to their house in Hubbardton, 45 minutes away, for the night. My train was two hours late coming in. There they were, in the cold, windy dark of mid-March in the north, waiting patiently for this teary, weary traveler. They wined and dined me, ran a hot bath for me, and tucked me in so I could gather enough strength to go home the next morning to face life alone on the other side of the lake. It would be a few months until the vacation season started and more folks would arrive to keep me company.

Chooney, you've been my friend, my mentor, my laughing buddy and an inspiration for my old age! You've made my life richer and more fun, and you've taught me much of what I know about Life. Thanks? Yes, thanks.

STOLEN CAR, VERMONT STYLE

WE OWNED SEVERAL CARS over the ten years we lived in Vermont.

I always drove a two-door car even when I was selling real estate. Four-door cars have always given me the willies. They're so frumpy. Somehow my real estate customers didn't seem to mind my two-door arrangement, and then, too, I always knew that the person who sat next to me in the front had the power to buy a property. Maybe not the money. The power.

Warren was a believer in buying used cars (previously owned! Love that.) Since he could work on car engines, I also was a believer in used-car buying. I have to tell you, though, that the first car I bought after Warren had died was a brand new Toyota simply because I didn't know how to work on car engines.

Warren had to haul stuff because he was a builder and drove only station wagons, but I always bought the cutest coupe I could afford. My rust-colored Vega (ick!) was the first but it was the best I could afford and the style was good, if not the color.

My favorite car was my silvery light blue Datsun. One cold and wintry January day, even though Warren and I'd abandoned the Ma and Pa Go Marketing plan, we drove to Fair Haven to Grand Union to buy a lot of groceries. A *lot* of groceries. Two baskets full. We walked out of the store and headed for the Datsun. The Datsun. Where was the Datsun? Didn't we park it here? Oh, maybe the next aisle. Nope. No Datsun. Then Warren had the nerve, the absolute nerve, to confess to me that he hadn't locked the door AND he'd left the *keys* in the ignition. I think I cursed him up and down then but I'm not sure. MY SWEET CAR! WHY? WHY? WHY? We had the presence of mind then to consider that the car may have been stolen.

We walked back into Grand Union, used their phone to call the local police, and they came within minutes. The kind policeman loaded our groceries into his patrol car trunk and drove us back to the Hubbardton Gulf, where we were living that winter. A dear man. He would call us if he heard anything, but our Long Island experience told us we probably wouldn't hear anything.

I loved that little Datsun. But you know how it is when you lose something and feel so bad about its disappearance, and then something shifts in your mind and your soul and your whole being? I'd gone upstairs to whip up a little something on my sewing machine to wear to the party we'd been invited to that night, and as I sewed, I began to think, Gee, if the car is gone for good, I could buy another car. Okay. What kind of car would I like to buy? A VW? Cute. What color? How about white this time? Oooooooh, yellow? Snazzy!

When the phone rang and the policeman told Warren the Datsun had been found, I had to be disappointed, didn't I?

The vacant car had appeared about three miles from the parking lot, and there were a couple of used wine bottles on the back floor, the gas tank was on Empty but everything else was in fine shape. Some kids had gone for a joy ride, bless their young Vermont hearts.

Goodbye, snazzy little yellow VW. Hello, damn silvery light blue Datsun.

Elaine Polson Shiber

BILLY

HOW CAN ONE WRITE ABOUT BILLY STEELE? One mention of his name and everyone goes aaaahhhhhhhhh! Funny, affable, easy-going (oh, up to a point!), good-natured and no task is too daunting for him.

Billy is a real Vermonter, and why did I think he was a Republican? I don't know. He never said he was and I never asked, but one day he told us he was a town councilman, and he's a Democrat! Lord, have mercy! No wonder we loved him! Right away he was one of us! (As if he hadn't been before.)

He took care of all of us. Every person and every house on Lake Beebe. And every person and every house on Lake Hortonia. And even if not everyone depended on him, there were enough of us so that his loyalty to us and our camps was evident. He was the man who plowed us out of the snow. We loved seeing Billy drive up the road in his black-truck-with-plow after every darn snowstorm. We cheered from our shoveled-off deck. He took care of our houses as if they were his children. Now he's helping his son Larry do it.

When we first met Billy he was married to Priscilla, and one winter night Warren and I were invited to the Steele's home for dinner. Smelled like pot roast cooking. I mean, I know my pot roast. We sat down at their dining room table and we helped ourselves to yummy mashed potatoes, delicious carrots and peas, a green salad, and, of course, the pot roast, well done. With gravy. I took a lot of meat, because I really like pot roast, and I was chewing my second mouthful when Billy asked me, "How do you like the venison?" DEER! Omigod! Tasted just like pot roast, but suddenly the more I chewed it the bigger it got. Could I offend these adorable hosts and not finish all that was on my plate? No! It took me a while but I ate it all, never forgetting for a minute that I was chewing on Bambi.

130

Sadly, Priscilla died within a year or two of our dinner with them, and Billy managed to endure bachelorhood for a time before he met Della, a nickname for Adele. We were invited to their wedding in 1981, and Della is one of the most "real" (authentic to the marrow was Della) women I've had the pleasure of knowing. She's pretty and kind and really downright loving, and has a beautiful soprano (or maybe contralto) voice. One night she played the piano for us and sang descant as the rest of us sang the melodies of *Amazing Grace* and *Oh, For a Closer Walk with Thee.* Della owned one of the first computers in my world and drove in to Rutland many days to play the organ and sing a solo at a wedding.

I cherish Della and Bill. They're my special Vermonters, and Warren and Bill were great pals. They wore each other like old shoes.

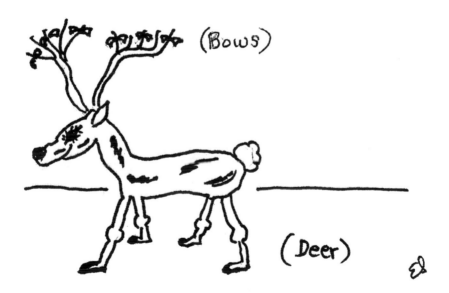

(Bows)

(Deer)

Elaine Polson Shiber

ANYONE CAN TAKE THE THRUWAY!

THAT'S WHAT I SAID OUT LOUD to myself in the car as I was driving to Cohoes to meet my sister Joan and her husband Bob for a day of fun and shopping. They live in New Jersey and we thought we'd compromise on the traveling and meet halfway and anyway Joan and I were born to shop and did it well together.

I was kidding myself, of course, about that thruway statement because once when Warren and I were going home to Long Island from Vermont one Sunday in the Corvette, I volunteered to drive the thruway while he took a little nap. I mean, how hard could driving the thruway, a many lanes highway, be, and just straight driving and very little traffic at that time of day and I can do this because I simply can because I'm a good driver and can be trusted to do a good job and let Warren sleep because he's been working so hard on the cabin and I haven't and he deserves a break, doesn't he?

An hour into the ride and I'm feeling smug, confident and almost comfortable and we round a curve and there it is: A BRIDGE! I could feel my foot come off the gas pedal quickly because crossing bridges had been one of my favorite phobias for at least five years and even this green one, which spanned the Mohawk River barge canal. It didn't rise and go down again like most bridges. It was just an extension of the road we were on so what's the big deal?

It *was* a big deal, and I yelled, "A BRIDGE! A BRIDGE!" and Warren jumped an inch off his sleeping seat as I pulled helter skelter off the road (but checking the traffic behind me first) and pulled to the shoulder and apologized to his ashen face. We switched places then and he drove the rest of the way home. So, you see, not everyone can take the thruway.

But I digress. I'm going to meet Joan and Bob in Cohoes, just above Albany, and that damn green bridge is stuck in my head, and that's why I said that thing about the thruway as I started out. Then I further stated, "I'll just drive down good old Route 9. It parallels the thruway and it may take me a little longer but it's a prettier ride, I'm sure, meandering as it does, and anyway I've allowed myself lots of time, having been up since five o'clock worrying about that dopey green bridge, and I'll be more relaxed when I get to Cohoes and we'll have a lovely time shopping. Joan and Bob will also probably remark on how relaxed I look." Sure.

So I did my meandering down Route 9 pretty as you please but did the map show by what means I had to get over the river each time Route 9 crossed it? Like, three bridges? And did I know I would end up in the city of Troy with many trucks and buses and commercial vehicles of all sizes and descriptions which can be truly scary to a fledgling country girl? And did the map tell me in order to get from Troy to Cohoes I'd end up high above Albany on a superstructure of urban renewal and be able to look down on that fair city as I tried to keep up with the traffic? I was that high. So much for avoiding a harmless green bridge. A growth spurt descended upon me then as I realized how ludicrous was the situation, and me in particular, and I started to laugh out loud at how funny I was after all.

It made a good story to share with Joan and Bob at lunch and when we sat down to rest after buying all that stuff.

BARN

AFTER THE HUBBARDTON GULF house had become part of our working family, Warren needed something else to create, and knew that since that property had once had a barn some yards south of the house, the Vermont grandfather clause would allow another to be built there without the state's permission. And this one we called BARN (all caps and don't ask me why.)

Once again the Fantastic Shiber Team designed a small house with one large room down, broken up by clever counter arrangements into kitchen and living/dining room, and a half bath. Upstairs became two bedrooms and bath, with a skylight in the master bedroom, which turned out to be a no-no because daylight pouring into a bedroom early in the morning can be an awakening experience. There was a cute staircase, with a landing just three steps up from the first floor and then turning to continue up to the second, and patio doors opening out to a small deck on the south for that five hours of sunshine and in front of which we placed our dining room table. The living room included a "bump-out," which we spotted in a building magazine, and it is simply what it is called: a six-foot mini bay window without the angles. It also included a one-foot by six-foot shelf which cried out for plants so I obliged.

The tiles surrounding the tub in the upstairs bath were a kind of light brown and I used the same color grout which I'm sure eliminated the need for a toothbrush with cleaner for years.

The BARN was a good place for entertaining. It was cozy and efficient when we had guests to feed, and we took advantage of these pleasant amenities during our several winters there.

We placed an ad in the *Rutland Herald* for a week to rent the Hubbardton Gulf house, and one spring afternoon during a heavy rainstorm, George Goodwin, who owned the general store on the east side of Lake Beebe, called us to say a young couple had stopped to ask about the house in the ad, and was it ours? Ten minutes later a tall man who looked like Alan Alda knocked at our door. He and his wife were from Minnesota and just felt like moving to Vermont, picked up the newspaper when they hit Rutland, saw our ad and drove the 20 miles to Hubbardton to look for us. We hurried them both into the kitchen, and after a few preliminary questions and answers, all four of us ran over to the Gulf house to have them take a look, and we made a deal immediately. Al (yes, his name was Al, but his last name was Wroblewski) thought that since it was the sixth of the month that the rent had to start from the first, and I said, Nah, it starts today to the same time next month. It never occurred to us to start out with this couple any other way, and Al looked surprised and probably re-thought his opinion of easterners, whatever that may have been, but we can guess.

Al and Delight (I think she was the child of a sixties hippy couple) were two of the finest tenants we'd met. We invited them for Thanksgiving dinner with us that year, and until they moved to be closer to their jobs at Killington, we saw a lot of each other and became good friends. Al made telephone reservations for ski lodges (this free spirit had once danced with the Polobilus dance troupe), and Delight eventually became the director of a museum near Whitehall. Al and I maintained a sketchy correspondence relationship for several years but unfortunately I never saw them again.

The BARN and the Hubbardton Gulf had several more tenants while I lived in Vermont. Diane (of bat fame) worked at Castleton College and became one of our tenants at the BARN. She moved on to Georgia and I've tried to get in touch with her with no luck.

Ann and Alan Andrews were tenants at the Gulf house after Warren died. Alan taught at Castleton College, and Ann was a missionary's daughter, had grown up in the Orient, and introduced me to the writings of

Frederick Buechner, a minister who lives in Vermont. I've tried to contact the Andrews, too, but my letter to Hyde Park, Vermont, was returned.

I met some special people through being a landlord and I'm sad we've lost touch. Memories are sweet, though, and will have to do.

BARN beginning

Warren on roof, John Gallagher on scaffold.

BARN Completed

CHICKEN!

I WOULDN'T WANT YOU TO THINK Warren and I never had any disagreements/arguments/fights/brawls. We had some that were doozies. One in particular I can remember with fondness because I did a swell thing after considering doing a dumb thing.

Picture a cozy, quiet winter evening around 7:30. We had just finished dinner. Roast chicken and half of it still sat on the platter. We chatted for a few minutes and then Warren got up from his chair and started to walk into the kitchen to dish up some ice cream which I knew he was planning to take into bed with him, because that's what he did every night after dinner. Then he'd rest the bowl on his chest and take spoonfuls of the contents while he read the newspaper or his current book.

That night, though, he said something, something about the chicken, I remember, that just hit me the wrong way, and I could feel my anger rising and I made some caustic remark, and he made some caustic remark, and then I . . . well, you know the rest, and can I remember what the words were about? Can anyone remember what a fight was about, ever?

While Warren dished his ice cream into the bowl, I sat in my dinner chair and slowly simmered and seethed but couldn't top his latest rotten remark. There was no snappy comeback on the tip of my tongue. Then he walked into the bedroom, calm as a cucumber, and slammed the door behind him.

I got up, picked up the rest of the chicken from the plate, held it in my hands, looking this way and that, trying to decide where to throw it. Ah! Through the elegant and dramatic 18 x 12 foot window overlooking the lake! I lifted the chicken shoulder height, like a football, took aim, and was about to heave it, when I thought, Oh, that's going to be a mess and the winter breezes will blow in. It will also be expensive to repair.

I brought my arm down and continued marching to the kitchen, still seething, and ah! the adorable 4 x 6 window over the sink appeared in my sight and I repeated the shoulder-height aim, and caught myself again (I'm sure it was the cold air and the expense this time and not the mess) and then I looked down into the cooling soapy water which had been sitting there since before dinner, and splat! down went the chicken into the soapy water, and since I was beginning to see the humor in all of this, I began laughing to myself and didn't stop until I had scrubbed that little fella clean with both hands rubbing this way and that. That was a good thing I had done (or not done) and not only was I proud of my budding maturity, I was pleased this wasn't going to cost us any money except for a new chicken. And we wouldn't have to put cardboard in the elegant window frames to keep the cold out. I then stuffed that very clean chicken into the garbage pail under the sink to get it out of the way.

The next night Warren was looking for the leftover chicken to make a dish with and asked me where it was.

I smiled my best fake smile and told him, "It's a long story which I'll tell you about later over cocktails, and why don't we just have a nice omelet. We've got lots of eggs."

Elaine Polson Shiber

THE HOUSES THAT WARREN BUILT

BESIDES BUILDING AND RENOVATING houses for us, Warren found still other ways to be busy which I'll tell you about. As we got used to our new home state, we discovered interests separate from the other. We still worked together when it was necessary but we could also fly solo. I remember, though, that as we performed our separate tasks, we never failed to honk and wave to each other when our cars passed on Route 30.

Not only do I have up-to-date photo albums, I also have a brief synopsis of every year from when we got to Vermont to the present. So don't mess with me and tell me it was 1978 when it was 1977. I'll take you to court.

So, one day in 1977 we bought a *Better Homes & Garden* magazine and fell in love with a dramatic contemporary home and sent for plans to build this house for speculation. We'd bought an equally dramatic piece of land from June, and Warren went to work immediately. He ordered building materials and had a load delivered as he needed it. He had tall, skinny, scary windows made to specification, and the day he installed those sky-high rectangles all by himself I went to Rutland for most of it. I'm a coward. I didn't want to watch.

I couldn't resist taping and texturing, though, once he got to that stage, and I painted the interior besides. When Warren finally turned the water on and nothing came out of the kitchen faucet, he was about to rip up the second floor flooring to get to the pipe when I suggested there might be some foreign matter lodged at the mouth of the faucet and there was and he thanked me more than was necessary but said people who aren't in on the actual task involved usually spot the flaw more readily which I thought kind of took away from his initial expression of gratitude but I kept quiet because, really, it was an easy solution to a hard problem but I'd be damned if I'd admit it.

Before we were ready to put the house on the market, we had one of our finest parties there. Chris and Grady had gotten married a few months before, and Carole had just graduated from UVM, so it was PARTY TIME! Friends and family came from miles around to help us celebrate, and Maris and Chick Ogg and family catered the eats, and we had music and danced. I remember particularly Jimmy Buffet's *Margaritaville* which my sister Joan kept sneaking into the tape player. We partied through the night and into the next day with a few hours out for sleeping.

I was working for Ida Young when we were ready to sell the house a month or so later after we'd cleaned up the scuff marks from all that dancing. We advertised it in the *Rutland Herald* and Ida made arrangements for me to meet Betty and John Moran at the house. Ida said, "Don't you budge from $50,000, d'ya hear?"

The Morans loved the house and were ready to talk business. John made an offer of $48,000. I gulped and honest to God this is what I said, "I'd rather have $50,000." He was no match for me and said, "Oh. Okay." Deal.

Before all this, and in the winter of 1976-77, Warren and I met Barbara and Charlie Porter who stopped in at the Whiting house while we were working on it. They lived in New York City and owned a house in Florida, and would we like to fix it up for them, all expenses paid? Sure. We spent two and a half months living in a motel in Tavares and drove each day to their house bordering a golf course in central Florida. Warren made some structural changes and I painted and wallpapered and on our days off we drove to the ocean and got sunburned and swam. While we ate lunch at the house, we watched the golfers from the sun porch and that's when I learned that not all golfers look like the ones we see on television.

In early 1979 Warren designed and built a house for our friends Luise and Wes Sheffield on Lake Beebe, and I helped with the interior.

We went to Florida for four and a half months in October 1979 and into 1980 and bought land in a subdivision and built a house for speculation, got pretty good at dealing with Brevard County's extensive building codes, and sold the house within a few months.

When we came back from Florida, Warren jumped right in and designed and built a house for our friends Marilyn and Ron Brostek on Lake Beebe, too. I had to get my hands on the interior of that one also.

He did some fancy kitchen redesigning for Ida and Jim Wright, our dentist and his wife and family who lived in Castleton, and he worked his magic on Dot and Ed Von Rhee's house up on the hill. I never took pictures of either project so you'll just have to trust me on this.

Warren had designed and was building a house on Lake Beebe for Mary Lou and Jim Broderick when he died in January 1984. It was in that house I last saw him before I drove to Maine to visit friends.

I've included pictures of most of these projects on the next four pages of this book, along with a picture of Warren taken on one of our trips to Maine.

**Warren
and the houses he built**

**Lake Beebe
1969-The first house built**

**Lake Beebe
1984-Broderick-The last house built**

Lake Beebe.
1977-Moran-Window Installation.

Lake Beebe.
1977-Moran-the Finished Product

Lake Beebe.
1979-Sheffield

Lake Beebe.
1978-Brostek-In Process

Lake Beebe.
1978-Brostek-Done Deal-View from lake

FLORIDA

LOOK TWICE PRICE 3 BR, 2½ bath & tub room, close to Space Center & future shopping center, open patio, garage, low upkeep, hand stained kitchen cabinets. $41,500. Call 269-2072.

1980-Port St. John

1977: Porter renovation, Tavares

**1977-Porter-Lunchtime
View**

146

AND A MERRY CHRISTMAS!

I HAVE PICTURES I TOOK at our house on the lake one Christmas when we decided it was time to have a Holiday Open House. That was 1983 and the temperature fell to around 38 below, and the thermometer had the smallest amount of red climbing up it I had ever seen. The pictures I took of our dramatic wall of windows facing the lake show how the frost had painted them as frost always paints windows on Christmas cards. You know the look.

We had a punch bowl filled with a boozy punch and fruit and a floating ice arrangement that was supposed to look jolly. The Benny crackled away and the sun had already gone down but we stayed warm with all those friends milling about. We probably had good old chips and some dips and pigs in a blanket and radishes and carrots and celery before I knew that was called *crudités,* and homemade Christmas cookies and cake finally and coffee at last, and I lost count of the number of neighbors who came in through the two doors and who didn't seem to want to leave. We laughed and joked and made Merry and I took many, many pictures and we called it our First Annual Christmas Open House.

As it turned out it was also our last annual Christmas open house because in less than a month Warren died suddenly of a heart attack at the age of 56 and I didn't feel much like having any more parties.

NINETEEN EIGHTY-FOUR

GEORGE ORWELL WROTE A NOVEL with that title and this is the part of my Vermont story that's painful to relate.

Warren died suddenly in January of that year and my life changed dramatically.

The man who was my husband, my daughters' dad, my friend, my partner, my lover, my confidant and my teacher was gone.

During the 33 years we'd been married and lived together on Long Island and in Vermont, we never had to hire an auto mechanic or a plumber or an electrician or a carpenter because Warren could build or fix anything. I never took that for granted. He was my dance partner, my movie companion, my cookbook reader and chef, my cathedral-ceiling painter, my ukulele-playing singer, my authority on most everything, my rock. He was my business partner, the guy who introduced me to Dixieland jazz and got me to appreciate Louis Armstrong and Wild Bill Davison, and the man who would try anything, except fly to Europe. He was funny and made me laugh. He was full of strange Pennsylvania colloquialisms that my kids and I still utter while our friends look at us in bewilderment. He could drive me wild, and he was so honest at times that he could also drive me crazy, especially when I wanted to steal a spoon from a restaurant. He was a loyal husband to me and a loyal friend to his friends, and I could trust him and count on him without question. Warren supported me in my yearning for independence, struggled constantly not to feel threatened and was finally winning.

He was my occasional door-slammer and my all-time favorite battle opponent. He was my match in being stubborn and neither of us ever apologized to the other if we could get away with it. I still dream about him.

When Warren was born they threw away the mold; he was one of a kind. People still say so.

I spent the rest of January 1984 busily taking care of what had to be done so that I wouldn't have to deal with how I could ever live without him. When the middle of February came, I flew to California to be with Chris and Grady. I had to get out of Vermont for a while, Chris needed help with her first pregnancy and we needed to share our loss. They comforted me as I experienced grief and loneliness, anger and fear, and sometimes all at once. While I wrestled daily with those emotions, I began writing a journal and found out how therapeutic filling notebook after notebook with my pain could be. I spent many hours at the ocean screaming and shaking my fist at the waves. It helped.

Of course——and I didn't know it then or I would have fast-forwarded the process——it took almost two years for me to begin to pick up the fragile pieces of my life, but that time in California started me on the right path. I even experienced the joy (and sadness) of holding Warren's and my first grandchild (the Dear Darling Adorable Darcy) in my arms before I went home.

I came back to Vermont the end of March, after a needed stay with Carole and her future husband Jim in New York City with *their* special brand of healing, and then I left them to embark on my sad and scary future without Warren.

I wasn't sure if I should stay in Vermont or move on, and ultimately decided that without Warren, living in Vermont would be harder than moving back to Long Island where I had family and old friends. It took a year to sort out the painful reminders of our life together, and just before Christmas 1984 I was packed and ready to leave the Hubbardton Gulf house, the one I hadn't sold.

A snowstorm was heading our way the day I left Vermont with Joan and Bob following behind in their car. We kept looking behind us as we hurried to beat the dark clouds bearing down on us. When we got to the split in the Hutchinson Parkway where Joan and Bob had to bear right for New Jersey and I went straight to get to Long Island, I knew I was suddenly on my own, all alone. The snow never reached us.

The next few years were the saddest I've known. There wasn't a day that I didn't miss Warren, his smile, his laughter, his arms. A memory of him would catch me off guard when I suddenly saw or smelled or heard something familiar, but more and more time began to elapse between sobbing bouts. Yes, time is a precious healer.

Warren taught me a lot about honesty and strength, and so much of who he was has become part of who I've eventually become.

Fifteen years after his death I started to write down my thoughts on our ten years in Vermont.

THE LIVIN' END

I'M GLAD THIS ISN'T The End.

As hard as some of those years were for me, I'm grateful that Warren and I had the nerve and the spirit to leave Long Island and take that risky leap up to Vermont, a state we didn't know, and that we had the tenacity to stay for ten years.

I'm a different person from the naïve Long Islander who smart-alecked her way north without a plan in her head. Oh, I'm still a smart aleck, but I have other sides of me that I like better, and I'm wiser for having met those Vermonters and for having had those experiences.

I'm richer because I haven't lived on Long Island all my life. I probably would have died of Provincialism because I was heading in that direction. And today, when I throw "I lived in Vermont for a while" into a conversation, they're impressed. (I never mention the homesickness.) I'd probably still be a sissy, too.

In the past few years, a friend and I have gone to Vermont to spend some days each winter at an inn in Quechee. He cross-country skis and I tried that but kept falling. Now I snowshoe through the meadows solo with just the bordering snow laden evergreens, the chickadees and the upside down nuthatches, the distant billowy clouds and my cold nose for company, and am overjoyed with what I'm finally feeling.

If no one is within earshot, I'm liable to shout, "I love this place!" When did I learn to love Vermont in the winter as well as summer? Ten years after I moved away, that's when. It's because I can leave whenever I want to and I can come back whenever I want to. And I do, as often as I can.

I think Warren would like that.

WHAT I FOUND OUT

NOT LONG AGO my daughter Carole and I drove up the New York Thruway to visit family in Lake George. Carole and Bill and their daughter Faith had moved from Brooklyn to Kingston the year before and were slowly settling in.

We talked about "settling in." We'd left Kingston an hour earlier. I was driving, but with one hand—the one I don't steer with—I was gesturing, and my right forefinger pointed diagonally to the right (indicating Vermont) and then I jerked my thumb over my right shoulder to indicate Long Island.

I said, "I couldn't separate my Long Island past life from my present Vermont life, and that's why I think I was having such homesickness problems." Carole asked me to repeat that, please. I talked around and around that but I had trouble landing where she could understand me.

Finally, Carole tried to compare their recent move with mine, and offered that Faith had adjusted to living in Kingston rather easily. Faith is eight years old! It's not unlike a kid sitting down and explaining to us old folks how a computer works. Quick, they are, and maybe closer to their truth, not having cluttered their young minds with too much stuff.

A week ago Faith had said to Carole, "I love Kingston and I miss Brooklyn." Carole jumped in, mother-like, and suggested that she probably still loves Brooklyn, too. Faith, with typical eight-year-old impatience and wisdom, replied, "Ma-um! No! I *love* Kingston and I *miss* Brooklyn. I don't live in Brooklyn any more. I live in Kingston and it's my home. Brooklyn isn't my home any more. But I *miss* it!"

Almost thirty years later, I get it. I've just found out when I lived in Vermont, it was my home. I didn't want to comprehend Long Island was no longer my home. But I *missed* it and it kept calling me back. I'd grown up there for 49 years and of course I missed it! I just hadn't done the necessary separation in my head. I wasn't eight years old.

The word "closure" comes to mind but it wasn't in vogue until it was too late. When Warren and I moved from Long Island, we hardly said goodbye, to friends or to anything else that had had meaning for us. (We were young!) No Goodbye, Long Island! No Hello, Vermont!

When I left Vermont ten years later, "closure" was one of the words *du jour,* and I was aware of my sorrow in leaving. I made certain I said goodbye to everyone I'd made friends with. To everyone I hadn't made friends with. I took pictures with a lump in my throat of my last views of the lake. I have a whole *scrapbook* of my goodbyes.

This was what I'd found out during those ten years. This time I was conscious of my teary goodbyes and the dread attending what I was about to embark on. This time I'd made plans for my immediate future: I had a place to stay until I found one of my own. I'd gotten a job so that I could support myself in the manner to which I'd become a stranger. This time I was ready.

No wonder I've loved Vermont. No wonder I go back and back and talk about it so much. It was my home for ten years!

Long Island is my home again and I love it. And now I miss Vermont! As they say, It's all in your head!

Thank you, Faith!

ACKNOWLEDGMENTS TO OUR GUESTS

BEFORE WE MOVED to Vermont, I had seen a poem in a book which I copied to a small card and handed out to anyone and everyone who had expressed even a small interest in visiting us.

Come in the evening!

Come in the morning!

Come when you're looked for

Or come without warning!

That's pretty corny, but please remember that when I copied it, I was pretty corny, too, not having reached 50. On the back I'd typed directions to Lake Beebe.

I remember names because one of my other endearing compulsive qualities is constant picture taking and a need to stick those pictures in photo albums. From the time I was a kid to yesterday. Albums all lined up in chronological order. My friend Vi Knowles told me to my face that the only other person she knew who was so organized was a patient at Pilgrim State Psychiatric Hospital. You can laugh, Vi, but this is how I knew who braved the rain and snow and icy roads and rutted driveway to see us. If I didn't take your picture, I'm doomed and I'm sorry, and shame on my compulsion lapse.

Those friends and family who stayed overnight were greeted in the shower by another of my famous poems. Our water supply was limited because our well was only 450 feet deep and should have been at least a million. When our first guests arrived from Long Island, where water is abundant and one doesn't have to think about its origins, and Warren and I heard the shower running and running and running and crossed our eyes at each other and turned blue with worry, I wrote a poem and hung it in the shower:

Long April showers may come your way,

But our well dries up on a summer's day,

So if you want to keep us happy,

In July and August, make it snappy!

The exclamation point was for friendliness. It worked. They understood. They came back, and took shorter showers.

Before I checked the albums and began the list of our guests, I'd forgotten how many friends and relations on weekend vacations came to be near us, to see us and cheer us. (And we made it known, dear, that we owned a telephone, dear.)

Thank you for your love and loyalty and for your willingness to drive those many miles there and back.

Thank you from the bottom of my Long Island to Vermont to Long Island heart.

NAMING NAMES

Here are the people who brought the longed-for stories of crime and traffic and crowded malls in the metropolitan area and spoke to us in those mahvelous New Yawk and Joisey accents:

Joan and Bob; Doris, Bob, Lynne, Sue, Rob, Jeanne and Michael Bruno; Chris and Grady, who brought Judy Ling and Mary Behrens; Carole, who brought Teddy, Mark, Pat, Robin and Loretta (and some of us made naughty gingerbread boys and girls one Christmas but who could be looking in the window? Santa Claus?); Rob Blank and Lisa; Harold (we called him Poppop) and Jen; Bert, Ann, Michael, Albert and Timmy Green, who picked apples with us; Joyce and Bill Houston from Amityville; Dave and Jeff (who brought his younger brother) Doniger; Peter Boeve, his wife and daughter; Lois, Christy (who helped me pick tomatoes in our Whiting garden) and Buddy (who was given a sun-catcher to take home) Huber; Mike (who made potato latkes with applesauce and baked an apple pie), Penny (who helped pick the apples), Emma, Daniel and Nikki Mandell; Bruce Spiegelman and a friend (who didn't like apples); Andy Jiritano (who danced in our living room) and Marilyn; Susan, Michael and Gillian (whom we took to a local farmer's barn so she could watch a Vermont cow being milked) Silver, from Rockville Centre; Nona and Bob Libenson from Pennsylvania; Maurice Troobnick (who sighed "whew" when he finally got to Route 30); Luise (who also danced in our living room) and Wes Sheffield; Vi and Cliff Knowles (two more living room dancers); Marilyn, Ron (who watched *The Nutcracker* on TV with Warren and me), Valerie, Bill and Keith (who gave me a plastic figure from *Star Wars* which I still have) Brostek; Millie, George and Bill (who hated our driveway, especially going down) Stattel; Mickey and Bernie Nussinow (who still haven't gotten over how cold it was); Sharon and Tom McLaughlin (who helped me celebrate my 50th); Grace and Hudson Clarke; Jeanne (who questioned the upstairs curtain-less windows and we figured she wanted no tall peeping raccoon looking at her) and Paul Royar; Dot and Karl Landmesser from Pennsylvania; Ben Brungraber from New Hampshire; Jim Griffin and his brother (who played the dictionary game by candlelight with us after the Thanksgiving turkey had been eaten and the power went off); Paul Ahrens, who was attending Vermont Law School; Rob Armet, who came over from Paul Smiths College; and Carol and Sam Wolcott (at whose wedding our four-year-old Chris was the flower girl).

The property owners who lived or vacationed on Lake Beebe follow in alphabetical order and not in order of appearance:

The Ahrens, Bitettos, Boilys, Bowens, Brandsemas, Breckenridges, Brodericks, Chapins, Clarks, Contants, Cooleys, Dellamontes, Earls, Ebbesens, Eldens, Fioccas, both Fleming families, Gallaghers, Gallos, Gralds, Gustafsons, Hubbards, Bill Jahn, June and Ruth, Kaminskis, Karps, Kowalskis, Krakauers, Masons, Menaghs, Morans, Osmuns, Paradisos, Principes, Pritchards, Pulses, Ranhofers, Ravkins, Rellers, Rounsavilles, Sondergelds, Tillmans, Vaillancourts, Von Rhees, Walkers, Weirs, Willards, Wilsons, Wolffs, Wolonses, Zeolis, and the Ziontzes. And if you think I left out first names because I don't remember some of them, you're right. And some never even set foot in our house or on our deck but God forbid anyone should be left out. (Do you ever get the feeling you've forgotten someone? Me, too. But I'll hear, I'll hear.)

Dare I forget Della and Bill Steele, Mildred and Vic Brewer, Shirley and Malcolm Vail, both Wright families (Ida, Jim, Julie, Mark and John) (and Marge and Cliff); Maris and Chick Ogg, and Jean and Ernie Palumbo? None of them stayed overnight, though, because they lived nearby, and they could go home and use as much water as they wanted to.